Praise for Leylâ Erbil

"How odd that a writer who first started making her mark in 1956 should remain a pioneer still today . . . How odd that, even after half a century, no writer capable of surpassing her has yet appeared."

—Mahmut Temizyürek, award-winning poet

"Leylâ Erbil is a consummate literary artist."

—Turkish National Committee for UNESCO

Praise for Leylâ Erbil's Novel *A Strange Woman*

"A brilliant and boundary-breaking novel . . . Leylâ Erbil brings to life an indomitable, big-hearted heroine in Nermin, a young woman in mid-twentieth-century Turkey who will do whatever it takes to write what she wants, fight for what she believes in, and live an unbridled, independent, and intellectual life. It is a great gift to the world that Erbil's radical masterpiece has been so beautifully translated into English." **—Mina Seçkin, author of *The Four Humors***

"An important feminist landmark." **—Rebecca Hussey, *Book Riot***

"Complex but fascinating." **—*The Modern Novel***

"A novel that plays with the limits of comprehension and communication . . . *A Strange Woman*, despite its seemingly prosaic form, weaves poetry among its lines." **—Marina Manoukian, *Full Stop***

OTHER BOOKS BY LEYLÂ ERBIL
AVAILABLE IN ENGLISH TRANSLATION

A Strange Woman

what remains

Leylâ Erbil

Translated from the Turkish by
Alev Ersan, Amy Marie Spangler,
and Mark David Wyers

DEEP VELLUM PUBLISHING

DALLAS, TEXAS

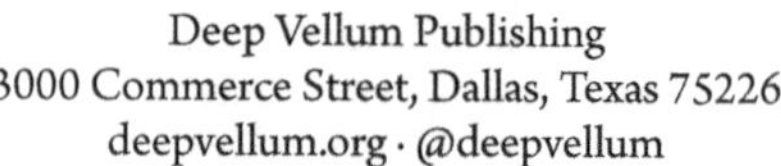

Deep Vellum Publishing
3000 Commerce Street, Dallas, Texas 75226
deepvellum.org · @deepvellum

Deep Vellum is a 501c3 nonprofit literary arts organization founded in 2013 with the mission to bring the world into conversation through literature.

Originally published in Turkish as *Kalan* by Türkiye İş Bankası Kültür Yayınları İş Türk A.Ş., Istanbul, Turkey, 2011

Published by arrangement with The Literary Estate of Leyla Erbil via AnatoliaLit Agency.

First English edition, 2025

Support for this publication has been provided in part by grants from the Texas Commission on the Arts, the City of Dallas Office of Arts and Culture, and the Addy Foundation.

LIBRARY OF CONGRESS CATALOGING-IN-PUBLICATION DATA

Names: Erbil, Leylâ author | Ersan, Alev translator | Spangler, Amy, 1978- translator | Wyers, Mark David translator
Title: What remains / Leylâ Erbil ; translated from the Turkish by Alev Ersan, Amy Marie Spangler, and Mark David Wyers.
Other titles: Kalan. English
Description: First English edition. | Dallas, Texas : Deep Vellum Publishing, 2025.
Identifiers: LCCN 2025019658 (print) | LCCN 2025019659 (ebook) | ISBN 9781646054015 trade paperback | ISBN 9781646054022 ebook
Subjects: LCGFT: Prose poems | Experimental poetry
Classification: LCC PL248.E62 K3513 2025 (print) | LCC PL248.E62 (ebook) | DDC [Fic]--dc23
LC record available at https://lccn.loc.gov/2025019658
LC ebook record available at https://lccn.loc.gov/2025019659

Cover art and design by In-House
Interior layout and typesetting by KGT

PRINTED IN THE UNITED STATES OF AMERICA

This book has never been submitted for any "awards."

for my daughter fatoş

thanks to . . .

rûken kızıler

özkan bilgin

mina bilauer

sibel cıngı

suat kasap

table of contents

INTRODUCTION

In the preface to his 1964 play, *Blues for Mister Charlie,* loosely based on the murder of Emmett Till, James Baldwin makes an unusual plea to his reader on behalf of the white murderer: "Try to understand," he writes, "this wretched man." This appeal to empathy stems from a recognition that the evildoer is the beneficiary of a larger system of oppression he only dimly understands. Society has taught him to fend for himself, to protect only those who look, speak, and act like him. "No man," Baldwin figures, "is a villain in his own eyes."

What Remains, the remarkable, experimental verse novel by the writer Leylâ Erbil, first published in 2011, is the coming-of-age story of a woman in a society convulsed by interethnic tension. The relentless pursuit of Lahzen, the young protagonist, to fathom the root of this evil leads her to scrutinize her own family members, the role of religion, and the fraught history of modern Turkey. In school, she learns of Sultan Mehmed III, who ordered the strangling of his nineteen brothers, and the oak coffins prepared for them in advance. Her widowed mother has taken up with a man she is forced to call "uncle," a beastly hunter who has turned their kitchen into a butcher shop. The newspapers report the abduction, murder, and bodily mutilation of a Kurdish journalist, and even Lahzen's rebellious paramour is thrown into prison for his political beliefs: "a crack can form between two things at any moment," Erbil observes, "a void no matter how much you long to bring them together."

In Erbil's topsy-turvy world, religion provides no solace, nor does philosophy. Lahzen's aunt urges her to have faith in the will of Allah, but he seems to send down misfortune after misfortune, and Lahzen finds the Quran brimming with sadness. Cain won't even bury his brother Abel. She peruses the copy of Søren Kierkegaard's *Fear and Trembling* that uncle keeps in his pocket, only to encounter a spirited defense of Abraham, who is willing to sacrifice his own son Isaac to God. "A nutcase," she snarls at the Danish philosopher. In a universe where brother has turned against brother, father against son, and the enemy can be in your own home, *What Remains* searches urgently for a way to escape these recurrent cycles of suffering.

Born in 1931 to a Turkish family with roots in the Balkans, Erbil mostly grew up in a multi-sectarian and multi-ethnic Istanbul, writing poems and short stories from an early age. Her father was a sea captain; in her late twenties, she traveled with him to the United States onboard a cargo steamer, which contributed to her fierce sense of independence. While at times darkly humorous, *What Remains* is an elegy for the gradual disappearance of that freely mixing Istanbul Erbil so intimately knew, a city in which the Saint Lucia-venerating Greek Orthodox Christian lived next door to the Laz people from the Black Sea.

A chauvinistic ultranationalism was chipping away at that harmony. The singular event that casts its shadow on *What Remains* is known today as the pogrom of September 6 and 7, 1955. When pro-government nationalists spread rumors that the Greeks had planted a bomb in Atatürk's ancestral home in Thessaloniki, riots broke out and thousands of non-Muslim properties in Istanbul were looted or destroyed: "we were kicked out of our country," grieves a Greek jeweler Lahzen encounters in Rhodes. While sightseeing on Nemrut, a mountain in southeastern Turkey known for its ancient stone statues from the Commagene Kingdom, she affectionately presses her cheek against the stone face of Antiochus; but her husband snaps at her bitterly for embracing a civilization that is not her own. Even the city gates and architectural landmarks around her have shed their older, foreign-sounding names; yet, bits and traces of this former past, what remains, keep resurfacing in Lahzen's mind, in the form of a song that fills the streets or in the memory of a now displaced Greek lover. She reflects that "the true locals are the folks buried underground, the ones above ground are all foreigners," declaring herself a stranger among strangers in her native land.

An autodidact, Erbil was an outspoken, politically engaged intellectual who thrived outside the academy. She left her studies in English Literature and Language at Istanbul University in 1951 after hastily getting married but returned to them when she got divorced a year later. Her second marriage to Mehmet Erbil, a civil engineer, prompted her to abandon her studies yet again, this time as a senior. But Erbil read widely, from Proust, Kafka, and Borges to Said, Hegel, Hikmet, Freud, and Marx. She was well-versed in the work of her Turkish friends and contemporaries, such as Kemal Tahir, Ilhan Berk, Ferit Edgü, Tezer Özlü, and Oğuz Atay. She seems to have radiated a warmth that elicited the deepest confidence of others, as evidenced by the many soul-bearing letters she received. Those letters are how I first found my way to her work.

Erbil believed that literature begins by looking, by being attentive to your immediate surroundings. "Masası cebindeydi," she once wrote of her literary forebear, Sait Faik, who upended the modern Turkish short story by training his gaze on fishermen, merchants, and laborers alike. "His writing desk was in his pocket." So, too, one of Erbil's favorite pastimes as a child was to invent stories for the passengers who caught her eye on the ferry across the Bosphorus.

While the formal innovation of *Gecede* (1968), her highly imaginative book of short stories, cemented her reputation in Turkish letters, her novel *A Strange Woman* (1971) was unprecedented for its overt discussions of female sexuality. In 2002, Erbil became the first—and to date only—Turkish female writer to be nominated for the Nobel Prize in Literature. Over a writing career that spanned more than five decades, Erbil rejected linear storytelling in favor of a fragmented and experimental style, in which the political and the personal were inextricably intertwined.

Alternating between past and present, poetry and prose, various spoken and written registers of Turkish, *What Remains* is the apex of a formally and formidably inventive mind. It is entirely composed in lowercase letters, and the most prevalent form of punctuation is a thrice-repeated comma, which signals both a pause and a continuation in the novel's stream of consciousness. Here, the reader will find something of James Joyce, in the frequent interruption of the interior monologue by the accidents of everyday life, in the forced collision between colloquial speech and the language of newspapers. Here, the reader will recall the poems of Claudia Rankine, in the way Erbil's narrative memorializes the names of real people who have been tortured or killed.

But the reader will also encounter Erbil, who resembles no one else in Turkish, or perhaps even world literature, as she forges a new and self-aware diction to give voice to women who seek their own pleasure, who read, argue, and think in a society that all too often glorifies female chastity and subservience as virtues. The older Lahzen, who is on a cocktail of antipsychotics, painkillers, and ADHD medication to treat an "amorphous state of existence," is the dominant voice, but Erbil freely dips into the speech of others with Bakhtinian verve.

Its breathless originality—compounded by its idiomatic speech, inverted sentences, and rhymes—makes *What Remains* a challenging text to render into English. Its translators, Alev Ersan, Amy Marie Spangler, and Mark David Wyers first embarked on this task in 2013 during a translation workshop on the Aegean island of Cunda. At first, they divvied up the text among themselves, but over a decade of editing and revising each other's sections, their voices have melded into one seamless whole—not unlike those of the characters in *What Remains*. Their use of contractions and careful attention to prosody generate forward momentum and a richly detailed, fleet-footed narrative abounding in musicality. Although Erbil did not live to see this translation—she passed away from Langerhans cell histiocytosis in 2013 shortly after the Gezi Park protests began—she would no doubt have approved of its ambition.

Is there no reply to the terrible darkness of history? No new beginning or state of innocence that can counteract our crimes? Erbil discerns that even children engage in "tiny acts of wickedness," which seem inexorably to lead to the violent acts of adults. When Lahzen forgets her pencil case at home one day, none of her classmates, save for a Jewish girl named Rosa, lends her a helping hand: "just how were they supposed to bear and raise / children for the spanking new privatized armies," Erbil asks, "women who wouldn't even spare a pencil." While mourning that general lack of compassion, *What Remains* finds hope in equally tiny acts of kindness, as when Lahzen's sister spends time with her reading Nâzim Hikmet's poetry:

> whatever you do, don't tell anyone, his poetry's been banned,,, when evening falls and we go up to the attic, she takes out those pink onionskin sheets of paper and reads

> to me for hours on end,,, I don't understand a thing,,, these poems are going to save people, she says,,, how, i ask,,, you'll see, she says,,,

Yet it is the almost negligible affinities between human beings, plain upon a closer look, that prove for Erbil an even greater source of comfort: "my love the lines of whose slender hands so resemble my own," Lahzen confesses to an ex. If violence is an attempt to extinguish what we think is not our own, then love for Erbil is an incantation against all sanctimony.

Ayten Tartici
New York, 2025

proem

in the garden rambler roses, slender thistles, angelica
scurl up every vertical thing they find
hellweed and stinging nettles
canopy two bushes
called gog magog
who whisper insidiously to each other
calling us "those tyrants"
a burst sack of charcoal
leaning against the plum tree
cries out in constant refrain; charcoal top-grade charcoooal!
the chimney starter
the grill
the gridiron
brass tongs
pine kindling
a box of *tekel* matches at hand,
the smell of tunny-bonito-mackerel entwines with the song drifting
from neighboring windows

yirise se perimeno yirise
mikrula mu kopela
ela ela ela...

there stands our three-story timber house
the work of a greek craftsman named hadji murat.

according to aunt, and according to uncle too—uncle being a man that no one knew my father was hiding in our house at one time—hadji murat was a master builder from trabzon who engraved his name into stone, and carved the arches of domes, a pilgrim to mecca, a christian in secret, a hadji in name. in the end he grew old; seeing as he'd gone to mecca, he must now be lying underground in eternal repose, coddled by his sire on high.

our house lies within the city walls that stretched from the golden horn to the marmara sea, built some 1,500 years ago by the emperor theodosios II on the historical peninsula, their opening ceremony graced by the presence of the emperor who made his grand entrance through the gate known as porta aurea. now stripped of that opulent past, puzzled vine tendrils on the west wing rise from the bottom of the basement door winding their way through wrought iron bars, embracing the columns, turning our veranda into a secret shrine. hadji murat must have gotten greek masons, christians in secret like himself, to do the stonework yet it bore neither their names nor the date. perhaps they couldn't care less about having a lasting presence in this world, was that it, who knows.

as the sun beats down, a feral masculine harmony billowing from the fener greek high school for boys, which was carved out of a ruby the size of a mountain in 1881 by the architect dimadis (it does bear his name), casts its lure onto the shores where our girlhood femininity begat of lust awaits, teeming with desires in fantastic tumult

eho mono pono

yirise...

from within that harmony a secret letter wrapped in the voice of efthim, son of uncle petrus, rises into the air alights on my sister's cheekbones rolling in waves of scarlet patent leather

as if she and efthim all alone at home one day

embrace for the first time

rapt in caresses

trembling, illiterate in love

on the verandah, our shrine.

like a resilient spider web this song resounds through streets and houses

from under beds and stairways

from beneath curtains and through walls

it seeps and seeps

into our young hearts

yirise se perimeno yirise
mikrula mu kopela
ela ela ela...

***

the fig, mulberry, plum, pomegranate, and sycamore trees, which look upon ayakapı gate formerly called aya theodosias, petrikapı gate formerly called petrion, and balat gate formerly called palation, grew up with these songs. insurmountable walls of travertine together with the bushes called gog magog protect the borders of the house.

with its rows of matchbox houses and narrow streets behind the walls, this place and the opposite shore (pera) shelter us, the people.

and in galatapera the remains of city walls are skirted by the seashore

and beneath the remains

further beneath

further still

nestled together, the souls of dead cities

leading down into endless layers of the past

this merciless city

assailed by our civilization,

considered both foreign and ours

both ours and not

bearing the soul of both above and below

and we its denizens wandering upon the earth for now knowing we too shall descend soon so soon sooner than a tick of cruel time

***

the walls of the city demolished in 194 by septimius severus—towering, dark skin, curly black hair—replaced in 326 by constantine the great who expanded the city's borders,

erecting stone columns on the spina of its hippodrome,

adorning it with hammams, sculptures, the serpent column, a harbor, even setting up a library, and it was upon a sliver of the dilapidated remains of this city that our home and front and back gardens were fated to exist.

the garden has borders

the house behind the wall to the north belongs to the family of aunt lefkothea, her husband is uncle petrus, her son is efthim.

our wooden door the color of rusted iron faces west and back

and forth it swings open and shut of its own accord

we thought it would topple but it survives still all crooked like that

the ground of the rear garden and the path leading to the front door

were paved in pebble mosaics

by the hands of an other

in the days when there was no need to conceal one's faith

the mosaics are flower patterned

some of them beaten, broken

when i was little i thought there were blossoms or flower seeds inside

sometimes when i was little if there was no one around

i'd pick up a stone and use it to smash another to pieces

but then when one is little

one thinks that everything contains something else

and when looking at the pebbles in the mosaics

from the balcony

the eye sees something else besides flowers

it sees bits and pieces of stories told

such as the one about baby moses

on the shoulders of a saint

crossing from this side of the water to the other

as uncle said

or the story of how he was found for the first time in a basket on the bank of a stream

the long slender fingers of the pharaoh's daughter

who found baby moses there and saved him.

one day i stole uncle's hammer

and smashed open baby moses's head and looked inside

my mother said to uncle, what on earth happened here

i know what happened, he said

but i'm not going to tell you

if i ever catch her in the act i'll smash *her* head in he grumbled.

the mosaics were locked in a tight embrace

yet bright green weeds still sprouted between them

whether or not i broke the stones

meaning

a crack can form between two things at any moment

a void no matter how much you long to bring them together

hadji murat was one of dozens of master builders survived by this lying world, yet no matter how many houses he built i'm sure that he was one of those who died having failed to seize his own truth, because knowing that others had surpassed him left him unfulfilled all his life just like the rest of us here on this earth

especially if we consider the pyramids of khufu, khafra, and menkaure from the 2500s bc...

* * *

“the pharaohs were simply fabulicious!” our history teacher said,,, time and again telling the story of the queen whose name sounded like achoo.

saying of this queen, “the obelisk she erected in her own honor in her own lifetime in karnak in the 1460s bc weighs 325 tons and is 29 meters high!”

the reason i speak of our history teacher now

is because of my friend rosa who i’d really like you to meet

we were inseparable from primary school till college...

why would i want you to meet rosa

well, it’s the idea that the essence of the truth of this text may have to do with her

though i don’t suppose human truth may ever be found, still

this is the quest i have ventured on dear readers, should i come clean

as if in confession

even if i’m not one to believe the words of confessors

and perhaps that’s what writing is

aware as you are that truth as such cannot possibly exist

not knowing whether truth may be found in the subjective

or in responsibility

or if it vanishes with the loss of what it means to be human

whether it stretches taut between your creation—your being—and society,

or whether it is simply found in freedom

a text woven of words

what might its truth be

what could the content of the text

the content of the text

the content of the text

be

other than

the writer in her own way

struggling to capture the truth

knowing that it cannot be captured

is the writer's truth

the text that she writes

is the truth of the text

the essence or

the substance of the writer

is the text of the truth

that of the writer

regardless

to climb out of this present

this well crammed full of doubt

into childhood

i'll take a ride

deeper and deeper

underground

and see.

***

when on that day rosa imagined the height of the queen herself rather than the rock to be 29 meters and by sheer coincidence our class mirrored the month of february being 29 in count (30 i might have said, yet best avoid the shadow of "si-murg") and those 29 girls all at once broke into a fit of giggles ducking beneath their desks

and the laughter of those 29 girls

made the hills come aliiive

with the sound of muusiiic

hopping and skipping

hand in hand with the girls' hearts

crystals of laughter

would soar above the waters of the golden horn

where at the bottom lie

the crosses of eastern rome sleeping

those warm, still waters of my childhood

as the slit between the brightening sky and the slate roof of our house

enveloped the magnificence of the bosphorus

taking umbrage at the laughter

of the hysterical waves

the history teacher

knocked points off our grades

rosa and i

in tears

had to resit the exam

as if we were to blame for the whole class drowning in laughter

and so we studied all summer long

binging on the episodes of our glorious history's past

an inheritance of bloodstained caftans

heirlooms of our forefathers that we tightly embraced

our elders expected this of us, expected us youngsters

to be in awe of our past

even if this rusted-out demand

weighed heavily upon us

our masters who

having set out from söğüt or some other far-flung village in bursa

raised the morality of nomad, dynasty, caliphate, sultan, *çelebi*

to benevolence of such proportions

as to string pearls onto beards anointed with date and palm oil

giving angel-faced boys a whiff

of the regal state of osman

of course our masters

having tasted the bitter anguish of war

would relish its sweet bounties

in their gardens resplendent with red-breasted robins

within the walls of seaside palaces

built by balyan effendi

and indeed they were ruthless to the heathen knights who stood

in defiance, guarding the lands they coveted

the sweat dripping from their brows hardened into gravestones

each a witness

to the vanguard charge

atop a white horse

gashing open the sky, hurtling into death

if it weren't for them

where would we be now we asked each other

rosa and i

we'd end up

like "cobbler talip"

we said

without a homeland, a language, a nation, without a past

not even a speck in the womb perhaps (i'll introduce you to cobbler talip soon enough)

but how come our sultans

taken in by the conniving two-bit coquetry of concubines

stricken sick with love

from arabia rushed the gates of vienna

holy sultanry swelling its vulgar force

as for rosa and me

hope buds in our hearts

that one day we too shall have

lovers who charge into battle for us

rosa likes them fair

while i prefer olive skin

by then i'm almost over my first love vangel

and his warm back

that shifted the lines of my face

when out of nowhere our master

hacking to pieces hundreds of thousands of alevi kurds or qizilbash—

our hair stands on end

but our master the prophet had a certain effulgence too

from our elders we heard

of his compassion how he cut the skirts of his caftan

that she might continue to slumber

we revolt against these hackneyed tales chronicled by our forefathers

against the power of reverence at play between master and slave
memorizing like hafizas
we said
ours was on par with rome
until the invention of gunpowder
an empire ruthless and elitist
masters
owners
willing subjects
slave markets
concubines
over time
capital and its slaves
the willing subjects of capital
slaves of the willing subjects
in fear and trembling
in trembling and fear
ahh the uncertainty of humanity's future
eyes dazzled
by the splendor of the executioner
much as we were blinded
by the luminous green of the jihadi mirror

take for instance the tireless conquests of selim the grim
from vienna to hungary
tripolitania to india
as the koran was recited in full
yes in its entirety
over and over
and what are we to make of suleiman the magnificent
slaughtering 25,000 enemy soldiers
on the plains of mohács
making a graveyard of the marshes of karassó
for king lajos II and the others who had survived
easier said than done
our hair standing on end once again
our hair rosa's and mine
we told our savage souls to cut it out
and came to our senses one day
imagine we said to each other whispering
as if the dead might spring from their graves
and hear us
what if they'd just made do
with a small piece of land
a piece of federal land

if only they'd been content our ancestors

with a cloak and a morsel

a cloak on their back and a morsel to eat

like our master the prophet (pbuh)

that exalted being

who'd made do with the camel caravans of our mother aisha or was it our mother khadija

why not take a gilded leaf out of his book

or

what if

shedding blood sweat and tears

working their fingers to the bone on equal footing with their subjects

the ottomans

had pulled themselves up by their own bootstraps

shoulder to the wheel

nose to the grindstone

at the windmill

like don quixote

whoosh, whoosh

my sister overheard

and snapped

pulling themselves up by their own bootstraps huh!

aren't you clever!

what would you know of the demands of war back then;

as if you knew the first thing about the desert

about lack

thirst

blinding gusts of sand

about hunger

at one's throat

or the morals of the starving

our mother khadija's caravan, pff

what would you know of fighting heathens

where would islam be without jihad

nowhere, that's where, we wouldn't even exist, not one of us

you'd like that, wouldn't you, she said, the whole world jewish and christian

she'd just started university

and fallen for some nationalist bloke

having forgotten all about her potbellied ex-husband, a man of the düzce gentry

and buried efthim, the love of her youth,

deep inside her heart

eyes full of rage

like silvana mangano's in *rome, open city*

her stride rat-ta-tat-tatified

but i wasn't afraid of her at all

trusting that she loved me

is christianity worse than islam sis, i asked

of course it is! she said

you talk like that again and i'll rip your tongue out

ours is the last and most glorious religion, you idiot

he who revealed our book revealed theirs too

ours contains the two that came before it

so you mean it's a knock off then

watch it or i'll punch your lights out she snapped

what did auntie tell us, that the torah and the bible were also revealed by allah

"and had allah willed, he could have made you all one nation, but he shall test each of you in that which he has given you!.."

ours is the final book

rosa jumped in

but wouldn't the whole world turn black

from all the black burkas binnur abla?

keep your kike nose out of this,

my sister said getting up into rosa's face

you're the one who made my sister like this so you better watch it

no no no no no she hasn't made me into anything sis, i said

how would you know who made you what you are, she said

her jaw set quivering by her nationalist lover's rage

how the hell would you know who's made you what you are

and with that she stormed out, slamming the door

we stared after her

then rosa said

she couldn't possibly know who made her the way she is either

true, she couldn't could she

then the two of us

at once

burst out laughing

she couldn't possibly know who made her the way she is either!

***

what i really wanted to say is that it was on that day with mister achoo

that accursed day when i'd left my pencil case at home

that day when rosa "crack"

broke her pencil in two handing me one half

saying, here,

carving that sound into my own personal history

laying the groundwork for who i am today

"crack"

a sound suggesting to me the idea of world citizenship as an end

how until that "crack" resounded

i'd had to beg all my classmates for a pencil

trusting them

each and every one of them

those sitting in the rows next to me

and those in front and behind

my darling friends

whom i always beat at dodgeball

but lost to at handball and volleyball,

whom i always passed at sprints

my friends

sunnis, jews, christians,

whether of the wealthy lower middle class

or future “humanbombs” hailing from the lumpen ranks

or beautiful poverty girls like fahrünnisa who’d wind up in the bawdy house of madame “lüks nermin”

forced migrants of population exchanges from the balkans who’d become m’ladies to wealthy men

rumelian refugees

girls whose families came from rhodes or crete

macedonians like firuze blonde blue-eyed salmon-skinned no stranger to poverty

dark-skinned family girls devout and demure like sümeyha

and secret sect girls like emine, suphiye, hayriye, hayrihünsa, members of a tariqa, though no one knew it at the time

and the grandmothers of those kurdish girls

who would become by all appearances militants

following the example of mustafa kemal

intent on building a nation-state

from each and every one of them did i beg a spare pencil

you know i would give my life for any one of you if it were me, i sobbed that's what i knew friendship to be

oh what a stupid idiot

pathetic girl at an impasse

upon sight of those hera-filled faces

confronted with her first aporia

i was driven to the verge

of no rien de rien

a crippled sparrow wallowing in self-pity

voice velvety

and they in retribution

from their screens every night for the rest of their lives

were doomed to listen to me

seething in their seats

i did in fact bear a resemblance to umm kulthum

our turkish teacher şahap bey lame foot false teeth

cane in hand, lahzen, come here my dear, he'd say and make me sing for them all

in the teacher's room

in the maqam kurdi muhajjar and the duyek rhythm

"my infinite sorrow makes my heart glad

you only you do i love like mad

i know very well

my fate will only make me sad

you only you do i love like mad"

sometimes in the maqam segah:

"before the heartsick pilgrims of love arrive at the spring..."

truth is any song they requested i'd sing

hearing it just once on the radio was enough for me

to commit it to memory

meanwhile as a guest student i was attending for free

the conservatory established by our republic recently

anyhow so in the wake of this horrific catastrophe

i turned to them

to my classmates

who had their eyes buried deep in their books

and in retaliation

i ripped off the latch to the gates of my heart

and flung it at their faces

at 29 sorry 28 no leave rosa out of this 27 girls

only rosa and rosa alone

how smart she was

saying, she couldn't possibly know who made her the way she is either

and that "crack"

riveted in my ear ever since

a permanent fixture till the afterlife or judgment day or whatever you call it

but now we're in the last years of high school

"hussies" i called them, speaking to myself, "full-blown hussies"

(the word hussy was a keepsake from our aunt,)

"you full-blown hussies you"

so yes we were the brightest girls in our class the ones least like the others

us two

rosa and i

they were sheep

it was already obvious how they'd end up

i said to my classmates that day (speaking to myself)

bear your thick-mustached husbands no fewer than five children

and may your tombstones be made of plain white squat-toilet marble

'cause I despise the plain white marble of graveyards

for in our house built by hadji murat

crypto-christian within the city walls

the toilet on the middle floor

was made of that very same marble

and on each side stood thick wooden sandals à la arc de triomphe and since that floor had no running water a tarnished pitcher and a copper jug hung

from a long nail driven into my nature morte

and from that day on i kept just anyone from entering willy-nilly for long stretches at a time

besides while i was at college most of them had already tied the knot

i never even saw their faces again

those spawning coquettes of turkey

and so for years growing up i approached other people with the trepidation of timorous trepidity

as if that hag sitting across from me would ever break her pencil in half and share it with someone else

thinking about it now though maybe they didn't have a pencil to spare

those poor girls

not so many feathers in anyone's nest back then

turkey's postwar push for progress

the days of the emaciated working class lugging

beams of metal with bare hands

men in white long johns

bearing massive sacks of flour

doubled over groaning

who knows how many hundreds of kilos of flour they carried ashore

from barges docked at the fener pier

one of them tipped over into the golden horn along with his sack of flour

just as i was playing hopscotch with vangel

and drowned before our very eyes

only after many years had passed

did i undo that latch

and fling it off with an oath

leaving ajar the gate of my heart for all to enter

just like that unforgettable oath theodosios II who'd built the land walls of this city

had sworn, upon entering through the golden gate

though perhaps the more appropriate passage to the virtuous chamber of my truth

would not be through the golden gate

but the "burnt gate" of the genoese

the crown gate of my heart

my god how clean and pure my young heart was back in those days

nothing like me today

though when I say "burnt gate" don't imagine

a gate of burnt wood

sure it may show signs of wear and tear here and there just like me

yet there remains an opening between the columns the blocks of stone a narrow passage leading inside

leading in and out

so that you may pass through

you and

herds of cattle, clowders of cats, packs of dogs, flocks of sheep

to the "other side/nether-end/border passage"

to "pera/peras/poros"

you know the way the waters of the golden horn rush like i was just saying above

how they rush to meet the waters of the bosphorus

that bosphorus bearing legends by the thousands

no no no no no i shouldn't get into that now

lest i tear you away from the truth of the text

but if i did get another chance i'd take it

i'd harp on and—

oh the bosphorus

with its thousands and thousands of legends

and burden of emotions embroidered

me onto my cells with fine gold thread

cross-stitch dense every hole filled in

with the colors, the depths, the scent of life its shores

down to the bottom of my "bosporos"

the "burnt gate" though surrounded

by walls of ancient stones

its curved vault

eviscerated by a municipal dozer around 2004

alas into whose hands has she fallen in the end this the world's most aged of ageless temple prostitutes

oh constantinople!

after so many justinianos and mehmed the conquerors just when she was about to become the capital of a global empire but alas!..

as for that "burnt gate,"

well, "of all that is left from the genoese, it is a finale superior even to the galata tower," semavi eyice says.

at the entrance

in the tympanum

above the lintel of the "burnt gate"

a coat of arms encaged

lest it be stolen by the poor and destitute

who encroach

scrawny arms outstretched

starving

the "burnt gate" with its coat of arms whether of st. george or andrea doria i never knew

look it's been right here all these centuries

go see for yourself

we learned about andrea doria too when we had to resit our exam

his 600-ship crusader fleet at preveza

sunk in 1538 by barbaros hayreddin pasha

that same barba-rossa

said to have written by order of suleiman the magnificent *the conquests of hayreddin pasha* the first turkish autobiography

though who's to say just how turkish he really was

no no no in this text i don't think i'll be speaking to you of that gate either,,, or maybe i will,,, why shouldn't i what is a human being but an object that's had the most abject threads of its truth ripped out,,, i might also have to mention the genoese colony and the raising of the "stones of iniquity",,, and their resemblance to me,,, uphill from tophane,,, downhill from galata tower,,, imagine the greater and lesser moat streets,,, the spitting image of me,,, how in the shape of a handheld fan they cast their colonies all the way down to the shoreline those ancient bandits and how they genoesified every place they went

with their slender streets

curling

and narrow

and here i go again with my childhood and my mother

her hair

not curly

but undulating

just like the streets snaking around the house where we used to live in fener

the scuffling alleyways

it was in the splendor of those knots

that ilhan berk told us about galata

how the genoese

surrounded themselves with their towers

and their endless walls of fear

against enemies that might emerge from the sea and how they...

o my dear readers, whether you exist or not i cannot be sure but if you do exist my dear readers

you can see i have a brain that i can't rein in

it's a bit on purpose perhaps but to stop this brain

my doctor wants to drown every last cell of it in pills but still i

will try to leave the writing of this text

to a troubled brain that knows no bounds

like a pair of bare feet hopping on scorching sand

to keep this text hidden from him

on the fiery sands of caddebostan reşit bey beach

we'll learn later that reşit bey is a member of the turkish communist party and behind bars but now we are little so very little in the hottest days of august

incapable of completing the story i keep you waiting

so be it we turks and kurds and foreigners

in this country all

made to wait in the lines of the ghouls who lord over us we're used to it

but anyway

what i mean to say is that it won't kill you to wait a little yourself

now to get back to my story

so i was upset with my classmates heartbroken devastated

by these girls i mean how on earth were they to become the republican mothers

of our republic

and the custodians of

my homeland

my tribe

my religion and my language

the language of our chastity

the chastity of our language

custodians

of the souls

of those glorious soldiers

just how were they supposed to bear and raise

children for the spanking new privatized armies

women who wouldn't even spare a pencil

that's why

those tiny acts of wickedness began to impart

like socrates the philosophy of fragile souls

the fact that what inflicts pain is evil

how it creeps

dawning vengefully in the sky

the dialectics of good born of evil

but let us get back now

rosa!

surly scrawny rosa

if she's still alive her lord should beg her forgiveness for all he put her through

after all he did put the poor girl through the wringer

the gods of that religion are vicious too

like all the gods of this world

surely rosa also suffered her lot of humanity's torment

brought on by the never-ending wrath of the gods

who despise human beings

though they themselves are human inventions

as i was saying we lost each other after high school

she was about to leave for israel

to perpetuate her progeny in the holiness of her land

she too would bear her new tribe children to defend its borders

babes circumcised on their eighth day

a new kemuel,

a new jacob,

a new isaac,

a hairy-handed esau

a dark-browed and blue-eyed sarah

a mute rebecca

a bethuel with a todo bara gaze

her existence would be a gift to the sons of israel that they might wipe out the people of palestine for good

rosa was fertile even back then

dancing the farandole

with her partner irfan

she said she'd gotten pregnant from holding hands

the angel gabriel breathed into my nostrils, that's how the fetus got there she said

no one knew she got rid of the baby

not her father yusuf the junkman in balat

who'd willed that his bones be taken to israel when he died

nor did her mother madam hirsch know anything of their dead grandchild nor was irfan any the wiser that he'd inseminated rosa

my mother secretly took her to her own midwife

telling madam hirsch, rosa's going to stay over at our place tonight if that's okay with you

and sternly warning us

you'd better keep your mouths shut

we're taking rosa's secret with us to our graves

otherwise our families will be done for.

her god gave her seven children

rosa

but only hairy-handed esau survives

his face forever turned to the wailing wall

the wailing wall

the wailing wall

my sister told me that when she was there

she asked one of the esaus wailing at the wall

what exactly is it you do here

duh isn't it obvious esau replied

i wail and pray,

imploring my god to absolve me of my sins

so does it work

naah!.. it's just a wall!

what good's a wall to anyone; yet all the same

so be it, my darling rosa my devoted childhood friend

if you're dead may "nurkalem" pencils

rain down upon your little plot of earth

as for me i'm still in this old madhouse

fit as a fiddle surprised i'm not dead yet...

so it was this very same rosa

who handed me half of her pencil right under the nose of mister achoo

and though that history snoot turned a blind eye to the heart of this richard the lionhearted

he never did forgive that virtuous act

nor the defiance it concealed within...

our people were full of wickedness back then

and though i may profess not to know what they're like now

actually i do i certainly do

and no i'm not afraid to speak of it

of our toddlers in orphanages beaten senseless with hoses at the hands of fatso jerks, little ones raped at an age when they know nothing yet of the world, child prostitutes pimped out, girls buried alive, pint-sized kids pummeled by the fists of rookie boxers at "nurseries of mercy"

not to mention

starved wailing babies grabbed by the legs bashed against walls

by the monstrous babysitters of this global liberal muslim turkey

or is it muslim global liberal turkey

the archbishop looking the other way

oh the iniquity

so here you are in a country that deserves to be paved in stones of iniquity

and how does one deal with that dear people

you tell me

after witnessing this parade of demons all my life

how is it i ask you

that i've not yet lost my mind

or have i

my current husband

insists

darling you're sick

am i the only one in this country who's gone mad

what about you

but anyway now rosa

she enshrined herself deep inside my soul

with that nurkalem pencil

of the diaspora jews

who loathed the institution of organized human government
and were tired
of being chased down
pushed around
on the run
for millennia
whittling nonstop they sharpened their pencils
a monument to humanity of sorts
and discovered
a vaccine
that prolongs the lives of our children
not to mention
a treatment for leukemia
and while you were going on
in that holy book of yours
about how "...the only religion in the sight of god is islam..."
they bequeathed to humanity
engels and marx with his mounted diamond
einstein debussy and papa freud
along with thousands of others
half of them beneath the earth
half on this terrain of earth water air fire

upon which we sway

and once we've made the journey there

we too shall become grass, insects, mice, trees, water...

***

i wonder did the owners of "nurkalem"
have anything to do with the "followers of nur"
or the jewish community...
no wait hear me out!
what with their kabbalah, their sefer yetzirah swinery
these people they lurk under every stone
and in any case are they not
the very same men who created
the monotheistic religious order that poisons our lives
even if our book
still says it's our god who revealed that religion too
i could never quite fathom just how
he revealed
the torah the psalms the new testament
before he himself was even born
but then again
though it says in the holy koran "...if god had wished he would have made you all of one faith; yet he will test each of you in that which he has bestowed upon you..."

so far the test results have been ludicrous

was it back then i wonder

that those radiant-faced moths

began gnawing away

at the roots of this republic we died and died to build

yet they say that the mullahs, sheikhs and imams of the time supported mustafa kemal

who knows their true intentions

or how they kept them hidden

from our blue-eyed giant

patiently, resentfully

till they'd wormed their way into the bloodstream

having understood

in his undeceivability

that passage would never be granted to the insidiousness of islam

or any other religious creed

they pretended to have been duped by his promises

and triptrapped him into the tanga of his tango

i "lahzen" who am i, what kind of person am i become

every day i ask myself where within my lived experience am i living

lahzen in which consciousness are you

from the clouds of which sky did you rain down

onto this wasteland tell me

seeing as the final consciousness shall be death

and the consciousness of consciousness at the moment of death cannot be written

at which junction of immaterial reality are you

i lahzen

reveled in everything rosa said

rosa, who was my best friend from that day on

rosa, whose face was vases of giggling freckles

it was with her i shared my everything

my secrets:

those secrets of mine

i will confess to you

like a true christian

that a strange man called uncle lived in our house

his face at times that of a workhorse

at others a hyena

and still at others angelic

a chimera of a hundred other beasts and men

who had a kind heart

a lived experience unknowable

strong hooves

i want you to know

that one night as he lay with my mother

through the keyhole

i watched them

that my mother writhed in pain, crying out,

but that my sister pulled me away saying

they're making love you idiot

and dragged me up to our bedroom in the attic

that many a night

a peacock tail spread across the ceiling from one end to the other

that i lay there till dawn counting the hundred gray-blue eyes scattered across the tail

that i woke my sister

sis, how do they do it

a man and a woman

and that my sister told me all about what happens when a woman and a man make love about the thrill of terrifying ecstasy

about how the pecker had not been hung upon men

as punishment to the opposite sex

as our aunt had said

on the contrary

by the will of god

its duty was to give pleasure not only to men

but to women too

is what my sister told me

much later after i'd grown up

and gained quite a bit of experience myself

i told my men that circumcision reduces the amount of pleasure a woman gets

yet again and again i was confronted

with a rage i simply could not understand

with a swift kick one of the most intellectual of the bunch

now a professor somewhere no doubt

sent me flying off the bed and onto the floor

when i brought the issue up

during our postorgasmic chat

i had other secrets back then too

like about how the cistern in the white marble courtyard

was full of egos

and that ego was a gaseous amalgam of us and god

the next day

i shared with rosa

all kinds of other secrets kids had at our age

along with my red nestle chocolate

my autographed photos

ava gardner

shirley temple

spencer tracy—myrna loy

my collections

my ramon novarroes

danielle darrieuxes—charles boyers

and how my mother's feet clad in red-heeled red-buckled shoes were swept off the ground as she danced the farandole in the courtyard

but the thing is

with rosa and i now confidantes because of that shared "nurkalem"

i became someone who had to believe

in every legend told to rosa by her father and her father's father

which she then passed on to me

my dear readers

it was as if i were repaying a debt

knowing that i forced myself into becoming a believer

unbelieving though i was

i began losing more and more of my own truth

through that mimicry of belief

i too believed

in the same stones she did

how despite their immortality

like us they too gasped for their final breath

in the early morning hours while everyone was sleeping and day was about to break

even before isaac crowed in the garden,

before waking up to uncle yelling enough already you damn bastards have some respect as the imam of fatih mosque woke up everyone in the house with his baritone call to prayer

even in my sleep i began to see the things rosa told me about;

yes the stones they sang they whistled

the giant statues guarding over "the temple of the dead" on the shores of the nile for example

whistled melodiously as the sun rose

those stone statues turned into song by the gusting wind as dusk fell—or was it the break of dawn—alighted upon my dreams time and time again

the song in the tale it turns out was an african king who had been killed by achilles

greeting his mother with each sunrise!

"god put bird throats inside those stones so the king could wake his mommy from her sleep you know," rosa said!

as if it were her own mother who'd been killed by achilles

my mother and i went to madam hirsch's funeral as well

a synagogue on raised pavement street

me and my mother

that too was a strange ceremony the likes of which we'd never seen but i won't get into that now wouldn't want to confuse you any further

besides i have no idea what's going on in your head as i write this text

the mind is it closed

can it conjoin with other minds of the world

is it hedged in by stones of iniquity

does it know no bounds

could it be any freer

and so rosa with surprising ferocity considering her twiggy legs made me believe in the stone statues that greeted the mother of the african king

by weaving me those long tales in the tubercular lily voice of "la dame aux camélias"

the same *lady of the camellia* published by remzi that put tears in our eyes when we read it at night my sister and i

but now we're still little i mean we've yet to read about that woman

we're little so very very little

and my mother she would go on and on

about how camélias was made up

and how dying of melancholia was stupid

but if you ask me she died of black bile herself—my mother that is!

for a long time i harbored doubts about how god managed to put bird throats in those stones but i didn't let on to rosa

stalwart as i was in my certainty that half a pencil is worth forty years of friendship

still when i got home i asked uncle that man we consulted about everything

the brain—or whatever he was—of the house i asked him if it was true

walking up to him one day when he was half cat half human

go on, he said, ask, i won't scratch

and then he continued, saying, of course it's true, surprising me, because he never called anything true that we knew to be true, and then he said:

after all god placed the voices of a thousand different birds into the vocal cords of that man you hear on the radio

who's that we asked

"and now some arias from bass-baritone ruhi su" he announced!

and with that he began

a rollicking "opera buffa"

turning his back to us

as if it weren't really us he was singing to

but the kaval he'd never be able to play

that he'd been carving with a dull knife for days

he surprised us once again

we stood there agape staring at his turned back

those years too would pass

when all of a sudden

bass-baritone ruhi su was kicked off the radio

by the respected conservatives of the time

turned out "he had the vocal cords of an armenian commie"

but still ruhi su kept right at it

picking up his saz and cursing them all:

> *(...)*
>
> *them who cut the wood for his coffin*
>
> *them who carried him to his grave*
>
> *them who spoke at his funeral*
>
> *and the imam's mama, yeah, her too...*

anyway i've gotten off track again oh this goddamn brain of mine

it can't be stopped

i should take my pills now hold on a minute...

***

years and years later at a moment when i least expected it

the sound of a stone

leapt from my being

enveloping my every cell,

its bitterish scent

climbing up every vertical thing that it found

whenever i saw it i was overcome by the desire to touch, hear, smell, call out

gripped by the sudden awareness that i myself am a stone

when stones from two thousand five hundred billion years ago were discovered

in anatolia no less

see it gives me goosebumps even now

to my lover i whispered i'm not human

these are the stones of god i said almost in a state of rapture

though i knew how the dialectic of nature worked

even at yay high still somehow i knew

that everything my aunt told us was a lie

that nature labored for who knows how many thousands of years to create a single one of our cells how many billions of years to mold us into humans

and who knows how many billions of years it was after becoming human

that i blathered to my lover, couldn't it be that the cells of stones have merged with my own

he told me not to ever repeat that to anyone else or they'd say i was mad

so i stopped talking

yet i couldn't stop myself from thinking

about the city stones and all the different ways i'd assembled them

about how the angled edges of those massive walls in peru nestled together without mortar

about göbeklitepe

about the ones at alacahöyük

caressing kissing gripping watertight

stone to stone

how they rendered impassable entrance to the city

and about those hands that wove the city borders of ephesos

stitching together thousands of cubic meters of stone into a tapestry

whose hands were they but those of assyrian, armenian, and kurdish stone masons of course who else

and i looked at my own hands

i thought of the lover i once had after i'd become an attractive young woman who took my hands into his and said to me my love whose palm lines are so like my own, don't go

dear readers sometimes we have days

when we don't know what we're doing

you know what i mean

i ask you why did i reject that lover of mine

who read the lines of my palms in his own

oh why did i turn him away

sure we're friends now

i've got a letter from him right here

i'll never forget that day

we were sitting on the balcony of the old park hotel

yahya kemal was inside at the bar

his huge ass spilling off the stool

i was too embarrassed to point it out

i couldn't help but laugh

i began cracking up as soon as he started going on about my hands

yet one more experience i've tucked away to add to the essence of my truth

one day

when i found myself in the hospitals of our republic

truth be told i do trust in turkish doctors

countless times they've saved my life
spending months in hospital rooms
losing my mind as draculas quivered on the walls
on the bed beside mine
was an old woman
forever clutching the holy koran
mumbling prayers day and night
beseeching god—for all muslims of the world—
but
when the doctors said there's nothing more we can do
you should come and get your mother
as she headed home dragged off in the arms of two sons
toward her final voyage
awaiting her at the port
set to billow its white sails
i'll never in my life
forget the last look
that poor woman
—who always saw me with a book in hand
and was surely fed up with me—
gave me
as she was getting out of bed

i tore open my shroud
and propping myself up on one elbow
i said to that voyager "godspeed, granny"
though to be honest i'm hardly the godspeeding type
but with me too being on my deathbed like this now you see
well there is a certain kinship that forms after a month in it together
knee-deep
side by side in the same room breathing
offering fruit to one another
swappingly like kurdish families exchanging girls as brides
so it was this same granny
who turned and looked at me
filling her side-eye with a strange resentment
and with the scant breath she had left she asked:
"so tell me, have all those books you read led you astray?!.."
for days i thought about that and laughed
i wasn't sure if i'd been led astray by all those books
why don't you tell me dear readers
can you-we be led astray by the things we read?..

***

and borders

when there are borders, there are enemy knights who set their sights upon them,

gates adorned with coats of arms, every rampart, every wall, every tower, every bastion

meaning thousands of hundreds of thousands of years of wars waged to destroy one another, of billions of dead nameless forgotten

the dust that rises from their graves

surely has mixed

with the earth

of socrates of athens,

with the earth of plato, aristotle, heraclitus,

of sina kabaağaç of konstantiniyye

and into tombs

by the millions

evidence that the golden pen

has imbued the soul of humanity

but now here we are

thousands of years later

a hundred thousand years since the emergence of homo sapiens living in a post-industrial era

i mean we've put behind us those days

when humanity out of hunger took to cannibalism

when butchering and eating the members of other tribes was condoned

having made it through bow arrow spear and axe

we believe we've gotten past those times

when life was a struggle of brute force against wind water and beast

like güngör dilmen's tourists who eat brains

at a live monkey restaurant

an age when it's said that if people go through life without questioning their existence

they can hardly be deemed human

that's why

when i visited mount nemrut with one of my husbands

i walked up to the statue of antiochus

perched at an altitude of 2,500 meters

its features hewn by assyrian master masons with stonified biceps

holding out against snow and ice

battling the god of wind

since 50 bc

and like a small child

i brushed my face against his stone cheeks

remembering or perhaps not quite able to remember that sweet-tempered vangel of my childhood

oh vangel

vangel are you still alive?

are you in athens

knocking back glasses of mastika

a few ena boukali mastika

don't forget me

say that there was a little turkish girl in fener

her name was lahzen

we'd slide down time-keeper street

on my sled made from an orange crate

he was my farandole partner,

together beneath the acacia trees

we sang

yirise se perimeno yirise

mikrula mu kopela

ela ela ela

my boy lover

i'm still a child without you i haven't been able to grow up

come

find me

on one of those days when we were only just learning to love men while dancing the farandole hand in hand under the watchful eye of my mother in our stone courtyard...

and then suddenly that man pulled me away from antiochus's broken nose and cracked cheek roughened by the ages

yanking at me savagely;

just as vangel and i would be wrested from each other forever in the wrath of september 6th and 7th masterminded by that duo adnan menderes and celâl bayar...

some think

we only live in this here present

that we've never been through

the paleolithic in 40,000 bc

or the neolithic

chalcolithic, hittite, roman, or byzantine eras

and my lover snapped,

"what a disgrace, embarrassing yourself like that in front of these foreigners! next you'll be slobbering all over king nebuchadnezzar!"

"but this is the immortal antiochus, not nebuchadnezzar?!"

"what's the difference, they're both infidels!" he said

as i sighed to myself, *long live* infidel antiochus, *long live* the infidel...

the static of my inner noise joining the shouts of "down with the government" i realized that i missed so many things

i'd given up to be with him

the streets, city squares, labor days, bloody sundays

the night sticks, tanks, clubs wielded by bearded men, tear gas, water cannons

amid the cries of human dignity will prevail, we'll stop the torture, we will not fail

that "crack" jolted my heart once again

so i got out of there

made a run for it

phew

with a wide open heart i strode forth

into the city's wide open spaces

onto its boulevards and bystreets

where revolutionaries awaited me

rock solid

left fists thrust into the air

but then how come

they've remained silent

our divine and destitute masses

tongue-tied

ever since

with mildewed eyes they watch

the processions to the gallows

lists of the dead and wounded hang from the city's walls

coffin buses plastered with photos of the dead

the saturday mothers

sunday,

tuesday wednesday thursday

no fathers around

friday the congregational prayer

the losses pile up

youths lost by the thousands

disappeared

meanwhile on television

innocent-faced killers

shed tears

mimicking the mothers of those they killed

they weep as they read poems

mouthing litanies of vengeance

meanwhile in the cinemas

the shenanigans of yeşilçam start to fade

the ayhan ışık, türkan şoray, erol taş mentality

the first images of us on the silver screen

and then there was

"song without end"

directed by charles vidor

depicting the life of famous piano virtuoso liszt

shadow heroes created

by authorities who've decided what is good and what is evil

bertolucci who did away with the feeling of shame

"last tango in paris"

getting to know greenaway

who spoke of a totalitarian superstructure

ivan the terrible

polanski

bergman

buñuel

antonioni

conductors of mass culture

of our latent morals

society

the people

listen to the orations

of firebrands

acclimated as they are to the theatrics

otherwise known as torture
a gaping mouth
orations
words
words
words upon words
the years ever more despotic and traitorous
replaced by their own replicas
reduced to fools the people cast votes for their own executioners
the endless screams
of the children of that same people
rise from the prisons
relentlessly
echoing
through the years
relentlessly
unable to say "enough!"
filled with a gratitude and reverence
that conceal fear
as reptiles of reverence
they will live and die
the newly dead just beside

holy shopping centers

in fear and trembling

like kierkegaard

spirit of the patristic age

wittingly stirred back to life

ruddy with joy

shimmying twirling

carousing cavorting

eyelashes fluttering

there was a time in my life

when men threw themselves at me

how they loved getting into my labyrinth from which they'd never escape

yet i didn't give a single one of them

the end of my silken thread

finally my first husband

who became my first husband because of his motorcycle

the sound of that engine

who knows how many horsepower

made my heart pound

along with the hearts of all the girls in the neighborhood

and on the back of his red leather jacket

that was like a smooth stele

in black letters

on red:

mademoiselle!..

my – concord – 6.30 roissy – kennedy airport about 9.30 yellow cab – to manhatten – sunny weather on central park. shopping the 5th avenue – flash at the bus stop – a soft drink in brooklin's cafe!!! champagne!!! preview at modern art gallery with my old limuzine – lovely walk along the city – back to paris then istanbul with tender souvenirs!!!

his body which i worshipped

and drowned in kisses

slanted eyes like those of ivan the terrible

carved into his impassive pharoahesque face

that man i put up with for the sake of that thing we call love

impervious to the mind gripped by the libido of youth

if only

i hadn't stopped bullhorning in city squares

for the good of society

he was the one who in the end drove me to say over and over

if only

if only

if only

take for example ioustinianos

who unlike empedocles

didn't throw himself into a volcano

to prove to his subjects

that he was divine

but rather

raised hundreds maybe thousands of temples

in constantinople

in the name of mary the mother of the son of god

by seizing upon humanity's mania for belief

he went down in history

as justinianos the great

yet in all my hypocrisy

i said to him

to that erstwhile husband of mine:

– do you really think life's so shallow darling?

– far from it; but you need to get a grip! you are obsessed with that boy mademoiselle...

– vangel's nothing more than a childhood memory,,, i thought i could tell you about him,,, i wish i'd never said a word!

– so why? why can't you forget him?!

– you tell me; why can't people give up on happy childhood memories?

– i said what i have to say; it's annoying the way you go around molesting stones! you're really starting to get on my nerves; even loving god would make more sense!

– is that all i am to you?.. you chewed right through my entire identity...

that's how we split up, my "*concord*" and i

wait no it's not

out of the blue he came back to me

my eyes multiplying with joy i leapt into all his arms

into his legs, his suckers, into the slippery vinyl of my octopus the fresh champagne of youth

cleaving to the mystery of life's unknowability

oh! how insatiable you are wrapped in the arms of your first man

the gentle trembling of the plectrum on your every cell

the most potent vulgarities spilling from lips

again and again mutually instinctively

the prophet mounting his buraq the two of you ascending

like lars von trier's antichrist

up and beyond the seven levels of heaven

but it was on mount ida that we split up for good

witnessed by that trickster zeus

only on mount ida was i finally able to wrest myself free of him

glass-green sap oozing from the vines

as masked bees attacked me

we broke up!

and what a break up it was!

later i'm going to tell you about that too.

i said later but

i'm not sure

maybe i'll write it as a separate book

that separation

in the form of a novella

i'll publish it with the title *a man*

yes yes

i'm certain

my mind is made up

i'm not putting it in this text

and the novella won't be titled *a man*

but rather *a strange man*

***

that's how it was

that's how it was this gaze the gaze of an unhappy consciousness turned towards another

a self still hampered by the forbiddings of the "unactualizedself"

the system using all its means to control existence

seeking to escape the inescapable

yet the immortal stones of this earth

have soundly crushed conceited time

indifferent to

the sham known as love schmove

that lord of desire

life's golden gates persistent so long as the earth exists

presiding over entrance and exit

lifetimes passed among its moats, walls, towers, street signs, obelisks

between temples

filled with the pain that awareness brings

above and below ground

the inescapabilities of uncivilized civilization

driven by the dream of a classless society

so there was that ash-pink obelisk

brought by theodosius from egypt

standing at the hippodrome of constantinople

that unfortunate obelisk that fell into the hands

of those grand times of tenses past

first raised in front of the karnak temple in luxor in 1490 bc to celebrate the victory of pharaoh thutmose III

and then there's selim III's archery stone

in a garbage dump in okmeydanı

and what about the archery stone of fatih

the one imprisoned in a scrapper's depot

beside a soccer field plunked next to the fatih sultan minbar

sending out mayday signals for years

part musselstone

part marble

bowmen's gravestones we thought immortal

once encircling the minbar

and now that archery stone

its marble its inscription alike

destroyed

the masoning of the ages that precede one's own

in those stones

the tribulations

of the workers and stone masters who carved the buttresses

foundations

columns

capitals

mummified time

reaching inside

sepia of its own corpse

caressing the hands that touch it

as if those hands were its creator

time as mummy

its drone

its moan

making merry

with the bloodthirsty villains of the time

and thutmose who had all thirty-one meters covered in the spell-binding names of his deadly victories

that traitor thutmose who said

"i too count as one of your ancestors you shan't forget me";

that pillar brought from alexandria to konstantinopolis

going all the way back to 390 ad to the times of theodosios

it waited

recumbent flush with the ground

in a corner of sultanahmet köftecisi

it waited for the hands that would raise it to eternity

and it was three thousand years later that the minarets of sinan too would rise in the hippodrome

grand sinan's

buttresses sagging on four sides

ruining the aesthetics of hagia sophia

his minarets taunting god

those stones—the stones of hagia sophia—

bound together

by the pouring of molten lead

condemned to immortality

by building masters named isidore and anthemios

that's right they would not use

pitch or lime

on the hagia sophia undying their names are inscribed

on the stones the arches the foundations

anthemios and isidore!..

how, you ask

simply by pouring molten lead

they stopped up the cracks in the stones

the liquid metal flowed finding the gaps and filling them in

the gaps between the stones that earthquakes, disasters, armageddon could not pry apart.

dedicated to mary the mother of the son of god the temple in question raised by ioustinianos on the ashes of the church that burnt down after the nika revolt...

i know i really shouldn't go on writing like this

at the speed of a thorn-trigger snaring a ladybug

here on this journey which truth be told i embarked upon for the love of stones

isn't that so my dear readers

there's this revolt happening now that i don't understand

soon i'll be seeing those people who blow themselves to pieces

i can't just ignore them

though i know that eventually every one of us must depart

through the rear gate of this caravanserai

you're speaking of children

who rather than suicide choose to become "humanbombs"

in the name of some unknown future

oh come on let's name it—in the name of founding one's own nation-state

but suicide was once a noble and personal choice

whereas being a "humanbomb" means being chosen

how would you know why you kill yourself

in the arena why

are all you poor people always down below

and the thumbs of those

sitting in the tribune always pointing down

you have other sisters too

pliant addicts of masculine fanaticism

an army of women made to feel ashamed

of their bodies fashioned by the creator

the paternalistic thumb

of patriarchy

bearing down on those poor women

those sisters of mine who've yet to learn the history of their own nature

bow down to their own personal behemoths

the lustful devotees of masculine fanaticism

consecrating and worshiping an imagination that's romantic

and parasitic

left over from the inquisition

actually i wasn't going to mention you people in this text

but i couldn't help myself

i know each one of you is a different desperation

what was it that plato said

divine madness is more perfect than ordinary human understanding

or could it be that i still pity you

you herds of sheep

is it even you i pity

or the adventure of my own heart

wasting my time on you for the sake of a dead-end desire

did you say pity

what pity

that's your hypocrisy

surrender disgusts you

admit it

i do

wait just a second let me take my pill...

compassion disgusts you too

compassion is actually self-pity

it is fear

you're fed up with being in this camp

what camp

you want to compare this place to the inquisition

but you yourself are ruthless

you have no pity for anyone anymore

but you just swallowed your pill

so in a little while

you'll start feeling like a human being again

who are you fooling

did you say camp

what camp

what do you mean fed up

you're here with your darling husband

he's an angel

your ex comes over often

they're close friends

what are you

you watch them

it's as if you're an outsider

you watch

like a stranger

your life reminds you of movie titles

but weren't you supposed to seek out the essence of truth

this book

began at a time when the world

had no way of knowing the word "humanbomb"

and what's more

yes go on

the mind contains no “dead souls”

or “achilles heel”

no turkish-kurdish war

we are little so very very little

our young mother’s suede shoes

cuban-heeled, red

propped against the lid of the byzantine cistern

in the courtyard of our house

uncle’s eyes

popping out from their underground caves

we play house every night

taking turns with the neighbors

meanwhile in the garden bush men called gog magog conspire

walls

we haven’t got a clue not yet anyway

about obelisks

the colossi of memnon

genoese walls

“humanbombs”

this is a society sick through and through

a society maimed

condemned even while living

to the torments of the grave

with the fear and trembling of søren

we look all of us together

upon this vast city's tombstones

with their inscriptions

their turbans

kavuks

sarıks

üsküfs

upon its artüres

and when i met this big-name collector

who at night would spirit them away

to his home

from göksu cemetery

and sometimes the cemeteries of

rumelihisarı

karacaahmet

eyüp

and sahrayı cedit

i didn't find his passion for stones strange at all

in fact i admired him

when i went to a cluttered room in his house

and saw all that he'd stolen and hidden away

ancient adornments from above the earth and below

phrygian

urartian

egyptian

sumerian

i said you are a noble soul

a conqueror of the underground

the lead dancer of labyrinths

you're the king of carnivals

ravenously he kissed my hands

gushing, you get me

you really do get me

then looming up with the might of a minotaur

the bastard set upon me

no i'm not going to tell you about that man

who are you anyway

yet again i digress from myself and the truth i'm seeking

whatever my self is

perhaps something i could come to know only by digressing

if you were to ask, what is it you want to write about:

– we’re here, this is the place

– ...

– this street

– ...

– this house

– ...

– these ruins of walls

– this courtyard

– ...

– this door

– ...

– still standing

– rotting away

– darkened

– rooftop caving in

– windows broken

– on the verge of collapse

– about to topple down

– gate; garden gate opening both in and out; separating each house from the other

– gate

of our childhood through which we’d step and peer at the outside world

yet we'd remain inside

forbidden

from venturing beyond that boundary

my sister and i

– ...

–is it really this house you're looking for

–it might be this house,,, the home i'm looking for on the pretense of finding one

– what?..

– i don't know

– ...

– the one i want to erase

– ...

– that i'm not conscious of

– what do you mean

– does consciousness exist

– yes it does but it's always changing, coming into being

– or maybe it's just always breaking down

– well not that it disappears, just that it changes

– look, the house is empty

– yes completely empty

– no one's home

– ...

– let's go inside

– the pebble mosaics, see!

– what a dump this place has become

– the front yard?

– the front yard!..

– not a single tree left

– they burnt them!

– how come the house didn't catch fire too

– i don't know, the trees were farther down, all the way over there

– and gog magog?

– they were in that corner

– uncle petrus and his family lived in the house behind that wall

– which house

– it's in ruins too,,, gog magog were at the head of the pack, they busted into all the houses at the same time,,, bush men wielding döner knives, sticks, clubs, cleavers, and korans. we had no weapons,,, uncle was already dead,,, mother too,,, the slopes and hills across the way were teeming with green turbans

– don't go on, i know the rest

...

– get out of here,,, this place is ours, they bellowed, driving us out,,, "yallah, yallah yallah min ruh, to havariyyun, to havariyyun!.." that strange language ringing in our ears,,, we didn't understand what they meant,,, an old man with a huge beard was beating the air with his cane, "since when has this place been yours, allah owns all, he's taken this place from you and given it to us," he was saying over and over. "he took it from you and gave it to us, he took it from you and gave it to us! to havariyyun, to havariyyun, get moving!.." boys wearing skullcaps and little girls in white headscarves brandishing thorny sticks drove us away crying out "allahu akbar",,, toward fatih mosque,,, where bearded men lying in wait armed with clubs and whips corralled us all inside,,, they were going to set us on fire just like they did to the people at madımak hotel,,, it was clear to us,,, everyone broke down in tears,,, we understood that it was the grandfathers of those same men who had carried out the armenian massacre,,, the bloodshed in dersim,,, all the atrocities...

but something strange happened,,, they froze in place,,, then all at once they unthawed and started running off as fast as they could,,, we didn't understand what was going on,,, they were unable to torch us,,, what happened,,, why did they stop,,, something had happened at that very moment,,, they stopped,,, we didn't know who had come and saved us,,, weeping we hugged each other,,, together we wept,,, joyfully we embraced,,, that's when i grasped the sublimity of weeping from joy,,, spreading its wings wide, joy reverberated through the mosque,,, it was terrifying,,, the joy of fear was so terrifying,,, how had we been saved,,, they'd left,,, they'd vanished,,, the mosque, which had once been the church of "hagia apostoloi," and after hagia sophia, which constantinos the first had built in the shape of a byzantine cross, was the "bloodiest church" of the byzantines,,, both constantinos and mehmed the conqueror were buried there,,, had they planned on burying us there too,,, that's how i woke up... out of breath...

– enough already, you go on about this every day

– this house...

– drop it, let's go

– look look the pebble mosaics are still here, that one's the finger of moses

– no it's not, it's a grape

– i'm going to take a closer look

– don't even think of touching it

– why not, zeyyat?

– let it go,,, it's all in the past,,, come on,,, you need to forget about it

it's all over and done with. don't just stand there,,, let's keep walking,,, look we have many long years ahead of us,,, i'll always be by your side,,, come, take my arm... my love whose palm lines are so like my own,,, i'm always by your side.

chapter one

mother and uncle were alive back then

mother would call him "uncle" and "uncle" would call mother "uncle"; they'd speak among themselves in a tongue we couldn't understand uncle-uncle-uncle-uncle...

when some of these words trickled into our ears drippity-drop bumpety-bump thump-bam-boom; is she his child his baby or his sister; is he her brother her father or her son? just then my sister would take me by the hand and pull me out into the garden; we'd climb onto the far wall where gog and magog stood and the moans sighs and shrieks of the house could no longer be heard and from there we'd watch the hum of the other city looking back at us from way over on the other side, the old rusty vessels docked and waiting at the shipyard, the industrial waste, the golden horn (khrysokeras) lying outstretched down below its horn the color of mud, we'd watch the sea of this city which uncle said was built of love, and the water still farther beyond, ever so slowly slipping toward the marmara.

the golden horn, water thrusts like a dagger into the earth at the end of the ice age,,, the earth parts in surrender taking the water in

the streams of kağıthane-alibeyköy-kasımpaşa surging

toward the vagina

our gaze would rove beyond the wall

we could not yet traverse

that wall

this city of walls

built of the dead

built on paganism

on christianity

and on love

***

uncle and mother were alive back then

after the hunt his kill strung up on his bow, hair and whiskers a bushy tangle uncle would go downstairs to the basement that was half kitchen half coal cellar, open the door to the backyard and release the hawk that stood on his arm as stiff as a pistol

but the creature refused to go

instead it would settle on its perch in the corner of the kitchen

sizing up our gnarled lives at cockcrow

that kitchen

a rectangularish hallway with a dining table in the middle

fifteen-candlepower lamp burning all day long

at one end abutting the coal cellar

rousing sighs of relief whenever the backyard door swung open

that rectangular kitchen

resembles the mirrored arcade in pera

also called the european arcade

looking down on us

from the alcoves in the walls

the first stone people of our childhood

goddesses

bare-breasted women dancing, holding lyres and sheaves of grain
from the walls of our kitchen hall meanwhile
hang an array of fowl and fish on hooks
in bits and pieces
cured
smoked
uncle
imagine
horned beasts springing from either side of his pitch-dark hair
brows thick as ropes
eyes white vortices
set to swallow everything in sight
upturned nose
mouth ready to devour all in its path
labyrinthine ears
long arms
fists clenched tight at the hip
one foot in front of the other
kouros
rails stretched taut across the chest
fit for the baghdad express
so tall

he picks honeyed figs
from the highest branches of the tree in the garden
when back from the hunt
no need for a ladder
some of the game he hangs on hooks driven into the kitchen walls
on and on he rambles about the hunt
the duck, the quail, the partridge, the goose whatever he's caught
in thunderous sentences
among clouds of plucked feathers...
and sometimes he goes fishing
and comes back
with a massive sea bream
as if he were kingfisher
or a wrinkly-faced john dory the size of a bream
(the kingfisher we mention being none other than horoz
captain of büyükada
remembered always
together with sina and selah)
or a flat-headed sulky fish we didn't know the name of
that resembled a dead lion
uncle
with the resolve of a monk of the inquisition

hacks his prey into pieces

guts and washes it clean

atop the kitchen counter in the basement

shooing away flies with a mesh wire swatter

he cures the share he sets aside for us, for the home

packing it all into baskets and canisters

then sends us off to take the rest to the neighbors

proclaiming:

"i made lawful for you the prey of the sea and its food

but the game of the land is forbidden when you are on pilgrimage" hah hah hah!

but people are starving damn it

like they give a shit what's forbidden or not?!

land, sea, sky

we'll gobble up anything we get our hands on right? ha ha haa!

then my sister and i

go from door to door

bearing sometimes web-footed creatures sometimes birds at other times hunks of fish

as if handing out

halva for the dead

like my mother cooked up every year for my father's soul

we tell the neighbors

aunt meryem, uncle ali, aunt lefkothea, mother havva,

aunt vara, the makruhis, uncle emrullah, aunt aliye...

"our mom sent this"

and they reply may it please allah

and when they say this

i imagine

allah

a cheerful man

white hair down to his knees

a thousand years old yet spry as ever

sitting cross-legged on the floor

eating halva

all by himself

***

my sister and i, the two of us

always trailed at uncle's heels

it was as if he'd whisk in

the ruckus and rumpus of the outside world

we knew nothing of yet

and lay it right at our feet:

come here my little starlings, come my little chicks

listen up

all this we gathered from the great deluge, the flood

take a good look these are from 3000 bc from the bogs of the antediluvian age

from swirling floods of mud

from the tarred waters of the earth

at moments like this, when seen from a distance, what with his posture, his stance, his face, his gaze, one eye slightly squinted, he took on the figure of john wayne in *rio bravo* yet when he asked mother to dance he opted for anthony quinn in kakoyannis's *zorba the greek,* it was obvious that he concealed in the depths of his being hundreds of novel and movie characters,,, but now we're little so very very little we don't understand his ways at all only call him crab-face behind his back, those critters we could never bring ourselves to eat which he catches and pops into his mouth with such salivating zest,,, and then there's the way he fingers the book he keeps in his coat pocket at all times to make sure it's still there,,, that very same book i'd delve into when i got older, the one by kierkegaard...

uncle rambles on, bobbing his hawk-head up and down

they'd even spotted a wild boar but it got away; in any case they hadn't brought dumdum bullets, or loaded the shotgun with buttshot, and nurettin hadn't brought his dog along to yelp out either, and so when they heard the boar's grunt and realized it was watching them, they reached for their guns,,, the boar took fright,,, not every boar does,,, and if it hadn't they would've been done for,,, but once that age-old image of man with a weapon arose in the boar's memory, it thought here i am facing death, my soul about to flee its cage; and off it ran in fear and trembling,,, the rush of its hoofprints, trembly like kierkegaard, taking flight before their eyes.

and when the boar got away

a primeval inner whistle

rent asunder a curtain of time

that's when

the hunters too were seized by fear and trembling

the very same fear and trembling of the boar infusing the natural-born executioner pores of each and every one of them

it took us a while to catch our breath but boy what a fun and exciting hunt it was! uncle went on, only søren would get it...

then like a man peering with astonishment into a microscope for the first time he looked us in the face one eye squinting,,, but you'll see we'll hunt it down we'll hunt that boar down for sure some other time,,, for sure, for sure, one day for sure!.. he said, stamping his foot,,, besides the villagers keep complaining, oh our gardens they're ruined in allah we seek refuge from their evilness; they've rooted up all our crops, come one day and we'll drive that beast your way toward the hillside with a blaring of horns and a beating of drums and pots

we'll hunt it down,,, you'll see,,, i'll bring you back a piece of him¡ his face scrunching up and flattening out like a piece of fabric as he spoke, his eyes now obscured, then glinting, glaring at us in a rage as if we were the boar that had escaped him; maybe he was trying to tell us something else in describing the hunt but what?¡ we couldn't make it out; we were little so very very little vangel and efthim still hadn't fled turkey, the gog magogs had yet to drive us out and nut-cases like søren kierkegaard hadn't gotten into our heads, not yet...

***

that flickering lighthouse,

it once stood at the bottom of what is now küçükçekmece lake,,, illuminating the waterfront road lined by the summer palaces of the nobility of constantinople,,, on the shore,,, illuminating the entrance to the harbor and the shallows marked with blocks of stone so ships didn't run aground

illuminating and luminous

a whirling beam lighting up its surroundings

hard to believe but it was a wood fire down below that gave off all that light

by the time neolithic remains were discovered even deeper down below, underneath the theodosian harbor, uncle and mother and our neighbors had long since passed on to the afterworld,,, and i was a grown woman looking at death from up close and life from afar but now we're little so very very little we know nothing yet of the meaning of lighthouses. we knock on doors and say,,, could we get a spoonful of yogurt auntie vara,,, mom needs a starter,,, can you spare a lemon auntie saadet,,, we'll bring you one back tomorrow,,, we're entranced by the starry language seeping through lives lived a-mingle, ours and the phanariotes' side by side,,, and by the tale of ego made up by uncle, spoken of in whispers from the belly of winter nights strung into one long creature,,, it was ego that helped auntie meryem give birth in a snap,,, that resurrected ferit the coachman's dying horse with a single breath,,, and it was ego that wrested uncle haçik back from the clutches of the police,,, and left kites at every doorstep for the children,,, my sister told me, i know where the keys are, one day when mother and uncle are away i'll open the trapdoor of the cistern and we'll see ego for ourselves!..

you keep going on about your small, insignificant life, but what is it you really want to say,,, a seam come undone, an infinite unraveling since childhood,,, this tyrannical consciousness besets you constantly,,, primitive shadows of figures on the wall,,, will you be able to unfurl that hidden thing, that thing your consciousness had concealed until that day,,, that thing you can't stand,,, what is it exactly,,, that thing you could never quite put your finger on,,, but always sought out,,, if only you were on a ship right now,,, on the deck, yes on the deck of a ship sailing against the wind, the sound of a bawdy seamen's shanty swept up by the gusting breeze,,, oh those open seas so boundlessly,,, "the ocean swells with my tears" a torrent of saltwater washes over your face which is turned to the sky as you speak with the stars if only at that moment you'd thrown yourself into the rustling water into the blue-white seething around the propellor blades,,, you can't,,,

***

lowering her voice mother says to uncle, why don't we butcher isaac? what's the point of having two roosters anyway,,, we've got ishmael, he's more than enough,,, sabahattin's really sick,,, they have nothing to eat,,, uncle gets up,,, hobbles away like a giant crab,,, why does he have a limp i ask my sister,,, well just look at what he's reading, it's a book about timur the lame!

who's that

an emperor who had a limp

you two stay here with your mother, uncle says as he heads for the stairs. we trail along after him into the garden,,, uncle is off to slaughter isaac...

isaac, isaac, come here, son, come my clever isaac! uncle called out,,, and then he waited,,, uncle's cleaver that he used to hack apart his prey gleamed brightly in his hand as isaac rose from next to the tent pitched by gog and magog and tottered over to him,,, our hens and our chicks followed after,,, isaac snuggled up to uncle in complete surrender,,, he rubbed up against uncle's legs,,, imagining he would be caressed as usual,,, all at once uncle wrapped his pincers around isaac's neck, hoisted him onto the log in front of the kitchen and lopped off his head,,, the blood on the knife he scraped off onto the log,,, ishmael, having witnessed it all, rounded up the hens and chicks cluck cluck cluck and made a run for it,,, what remained of isaac came tumbling down before us the dead body headless then threw itself into the air it leapt up

lurched to the left then to the right

back up into the air again

mustering its eyes onto its tail it stared us down

put my head back on it said

and then finally in a feat of incredible strength it got up

strode forth headless

stopped right in front of uncle

began to spin around

kicking up a storm of dust

round and round it spun

until it fell flat onto the ground

what remained on the earth

were the scarlet ripples

of a stone tossed into the sea

its beak

its comb

face and eyes

implored us all the while

from the other side of the log

my sister and i the two of us

we saw everything that happened

our eyes clenched shut

we asked how on earth our mother

could be with this murderer

this vile man—how?..

and on that day we hung isaac's bloody amulet

around our own necks

and on that day uncle strutted around the house like the hero

who'd slayed the minotaur and rested atop its body

but now we are little so very very little we know nothing yet of the minotaur nor of theseus...

***

our house stood north of the border marking the plot bestowed by mehmed the conqueror upon "the greek subjects" proclaiming "this bit belongs to the greeks" and its southern intersection upon lands bestowed by no one, fossilized civilizations, lands in ruin, much like a scarecrow it faced north and south and east where in winter the northwesterly wind blustered and storm petrels bandit observatory of the skies would plunge in one end and come out the other screeching but it overlooked the sea.

actually there are no borders in fener; they're all buried underground

the remnants of narrow streets where we've lived for millennia roots ensnared in the earth nestled together

with the severed heads

of animals turned to pulp their tails, horns, sexual organs in tatters debris of churches, rubble of domes, tomb spiders, clotted up bathhouses; muhlio, the thirteenth century church of st. mary of the mongols built by maria palaiologina now stands on hairpin-maker street, then there's brick-maker avenue which is pretty much the same as dignatary school street and grass street meanwhile yıldırım türk and abdülezelpaşa avenues join forces to gang up on the patriarchate, wooden minaret street has chopped off the head of vidinian; vidinian and brick-maker suffocate strumica, but most importantly every street every act awaits the day of its resurrection, and thus do we find ourselves in the midst of pandemonium from zamboğlu, masnavi school street, tobacconist, standard-bearer, broken water pump, no horses, all the way up to miniaturist haydar yet fener still looks towards the light; the sea! iodine is a sacred relic that rocks our hammock with the mythic breeze drawn from the bottomless layers of the golden horn

then there's fener pier avenue and its square standing at their own qibla for so many moons marking the point of freedom's escape but arrival too because the sea the sea! again the sea! washing its coastal veil ever since its creation

it writhes within purging the earth's black blood

and with its labyrinths that clamber back to itself

it wrenches the waves from its womb

and heaves itself into the marmara

as for the fish

fish of two millennia sneak in from under unkapanı bridge, the last great-grandspawn of the fish that were the livelihood of our byzantine kin we go down to the neighborhood at the very bottom giddy as we ride in carriages made of moss looking up at galata tower as if we might live as long as it we couldn't be happier sometimes in the hours when the misty foggy light dissolves with grief or when the crimson wings of the sun spread across the tower's realm just as the arrow slits squint dazzled by the carmine, that's when we head down the whole neighborhood together to go fishing in nova roma.

we'll crowd the shoreline each household fishing nets in one hand and in the other wicker baskets, tins, and crates to stuff the fish into; on the shores of the golden horn thick with seagrass and sea peony lampshades, we, the people, all of us pile alongside one another young and old shoulder to shoulder, in a single swoop we fill our nets to the brim with the wriggling bonito and mackerel that swim right up to our feet, then carrying our tins, baskets, and crates, we cheerfully begin making our way back home.

as we huff and puff our way up the hill an army of cats, awfully greedy, meowing impatiently, trail after us snatching the fish that flop out of our crates; just like the fish still alive in their stomachs they jump up and down till they puke while the kittens amongst them hiccup and fall to the ground in a gorged stupor.

this abundance that satiates both the rich and the poor is called "the table of jesus christ" each household will have a feast for themselves that evening

did you know my dear readers that there's also "the cradle of jesus christ" in istanbul just as famed as "the table of jesus christ"; it's in the hagia sophia—aunt lefkothea secretly took raggedy mefkûre there to cure her of idiocy

raggedy did get her wits back for a while, having been absolved of her mother's sins; a mother's sins all of them are passed on to her daughter aunt lefkothea had professed in the eastern wing of the upper gallery in hagia sophia there stands a cradle of red marble; it is said that crippled children born to sinful mothers shall be healed if they are bathed in it, and what's more "jesus christ's very own baptismal font" stands in a corner near the red cradle in hagia sophia; in which he was baptized after being born to the virgin mother mary.

it is said that emperor constantine had the cradle brought to istanbul from bethlehem... a world-renowned cradle of stone, of it the late evliya çelebi is said to have said, "when wicked children are bathed in it the blood of christ merges with their own and they become virtuous i saw it with my own eyes."

***

before reaching our house, as you walk down from standard-bearer slope, you arrive at the greek high school for boys (ecole grecque garçons—yoakimiyon—), the "mega school!" as we used to call it, its bricks the color of the blood of pallid popes, the work of architect dimadis. across from it standing on dignitary school street, hidden behind high walls is the greek high school for girls (ecole grecque filles—yoakimiyon—) which for some reason was not graced with the same magnificence as the boys' school. turn onto grass street and directly across from the church of virgin mary stands a row of seven matchbox houses all side by side including the home of uncle emrullah effendi who worked for monsieur garbis as a baster, then uncle kosta the butcher, a karamanid turk who worked at the slaughterhouse in sütlüce, his wife aunt vara sent us sweetbreads with vangel

on the way to fatih the house of raggedy mefkûre's father, uncle ferit the coachman, and aunt meryem, bay window and all... efthim's father uncle petrus the draper, his wife, my mother's dear friend, our "auntie roly-poly" auntie lefkothea, our backyard neighbors, their backyard a patchwork of flower beds, behind which efthim had kissed my sister,,, i saw them,,, auntie aliye, one of the women who rolled tobacco at the cibali factory

looking after her husband uncle şakir the paralytic paralyzed by a stroke

yet reciting the koran from where he lay

his deep voice

making the heavens of the heavens rumble

then there was uncle haçik father of mesrop who had a furniture workshop in pera on kallavi street, who was later beaten during the pogrom of september 6th and 7th left crippled then bedridden.

monsieur garbis a tailor for wealthy greek families, his wife alis hanım went about dressed only in black, their house though was the color of indigo. farther down along the shore no more mansions remained. the bulgarian church was one of the most dazzling in fener what with its handsome priests. in and around fener, there remained but a few families who were the last remnants of that class known as the "greek petite bourgeoisie" the meaning of which we didn't know at the time... you could count on one hand the number of turks living there; like us they were frayed and tattered, most of them quietly toiling away as toymakers in eyüp,,, in fact apart from a few families the greeks also grew up poor just like us but we weren't aware of this inequality not yet. singing and dancing drove away those feelings of lack. songs were everything; in every house a different voice:

"yirise..." "night and day..." "c'est si bon..." "ayrılık belki ölümden beter..."

at the time my sister was teaching english to raggedy mefkûre who would flip her skirt and shout "i am glad i meet you!!!" in the street as she danced at the doorsteps of houses. people who saw her laughed saying raggedy's caught the farandole bug again...

the story goes that the farandole was passed down by my grandmother and that it was my mother who made it popular in our neighborhood. in fact it's an old greek dance. but hardly any of its greekness was left by the time it reached us; we children transformed the farandole into a dance that was in turn erotic, narcissistic, masochistic, aggressive, passive, or exhibitionist depending upon our particular inherent characters, temperaments, and copycatting proclivities.

you keep going on and on; are these the things you really want to say,,, you have no idea where you're going with all of this? there's something you expect of your childhood! is it from childhood that you hope to glean the essence of truth?.. the essence utterance substance appearance of truth; is truth something static, something that waits,,, truth is that which allows us to make life a part of ourselves søren said,,, stop wandering these dead-end streets,,, rest a while,,, you're sick take your pills...

***

dear readers i'd like to explain why i called søren kierkegaard a nutcase earlier,,, though how it is my readers are "dear" i do not know,,, maybe because the thought of uncle got me going again,,, or maybe:

because while interpreting prophet abraham's sacrifice of his son to god søren determined that "the dialectic of faith is the most refined and most remarkable of all",,,

now a—prophet—is going to butcher an innocent boy

why

to curry favor with god

out of his passion for god

or was it fear

time and again we listened to that tale punctuated by the clickety-clack melody of my aunt's false teeth back in those difficult days when childhood strove to comprehend the universe

those difficult days

when we didn't know in which direction we'd head

what kind of world we lived in

who we were

why we'd come into the world

why there was all this living and dying for no apparent reason when we weren't even the ones who'd wanted to come into this world in the first place

shuddering we'd listen

to the story of the father who was going to kill isaac

while knitting a wool cardigan she never finished

our aunt

would mutter that it was a sin to ask about things only god knows

that his commands must be respectfully followed

that the mind can never know anything

clacking her knitting needles together with crab-like thrusts she'd endlessly recite the words of allah:

"let there be no doubt that allah (jalla jalaluhu)—click click click,,, clack clickety click—,,, is all-knowing,,, blessing and smiting whomever he desires,,, -click clack click- there is but one god for us all; there is no other god, only him! he, the most gracious the most merciful,,, allah is omnipotent,,, all-knowing and powerful..."

yet as if i carried within me

a religion kept secret from my aunt

fearfully

i questioned at every opportunity

why a father would butcher his son

when i escaped from between aunt's knitting needles

and came across him in uncle's søren

we first heard about søren from that dragon known as uncle

gotcha! i said to søren

at the foot of gog magog

or leaning against

the wire fence of the coop

immersed in the sweet chirruping of chicks

sometimes while floating on my back in the sea lost in the sky in the thousand shades of blue swept in by the wind

whenever i was alone

in marriage, abortion, university, divorce, remarriage, the times in between

and especially in that cold mosque where prayers were read after burying my mom and uncle

in the dead of winter

now i've caught you alone søren, i said

the act of thinking

is a kind of pain that seeps from the full moon peering down like cold glass,

and moans quietly to itself "cogitatio, cogitatio" you know what i mean

in any case this text is more or less dedicated to the prophet abraham, whom søren defended, and his son isaac

whenever we'd glance around

at the screaming children, the crowds of women and men

and be on the verge of protest

against how allah didn't love us humans

how he chuckled as he mocked us

forever making us grapple with wars, sickness, and evil

despite his power to do as he pleased

my aunt would tell us:

clear your mind of doubt

for he knows who doubts him

and punishes them

you mustn't ask him questions

"verily there were others before you

who asked such questions

and in consequence became infidels..."

uncle, what's an infidel?

"someone who denies the existence of allah,

but it doesn't matter 'cause his existence is nothing but a rumor anyhow!"

my sister said, i'm gonna tell auntie on you! rumors are a bad thing right?

of course they're bad what did you think! they're really bad!

give my best to the old hag

what does rumor mean i asked my sister

it's something like gossip, she said.

***

our aunt takes us to göksu creek, to the picnic grounds in dört kardeşler to have lemon soda, to the fairgrounds on the first sunday of september, to drink from the healing waters of holy springs, to listen to the hurdy-gurdy player, to watch the syrtaki dancers. though gnarled and knurly she is light on her feet; we spend much of our summer vacations at her place.

seated on her throne, our aunt delivers lectures about how girls are supposed to sit. putting down her knitting needles she squeezes together her legs which are swollen like balloons tucking her skirt neatly between her thighs and the seat of the sofa and says, go on, try it. and when you're picking something up from the floor don't go sticking your butt up in the air, instead kneel down to one side! your turn now girls! you first young lady, go on, from where you're sitting! but auntie how, my feet won't even touch the floor?.. it doesn't matter just make sure your legs are pressed together; keep practicing or else. no buggy ride till you get it right!..

the buggy is a rectangularish wooden vehicle pulled by a single horse. uncle hasan runs tralala up to the buggy. tralala and i get on really well. she whinnies when she sees me and i reach up to the highest elevation i can and stroke her red coat. her haunches are strong and her legs are slender. the way into the buggy is through flaps in the rear that swing open and shut like saloon doors. black wax-cloth seats on each side, an oil-painted mural on the ceiling; the eye looks up from the lush vernal green of küçüksu meadow, the inspiration for the mural, to take in the light of the sea reflecting off the dark woods of rumeli cemetery. the same light that gleams from the lower leaves of the artist constable's olive trees. but now we are young so very very young and know nothing yet of constable or of the silvery green undersides of leaves... we know that there is no seat in the space behind the driver and that the buggy and the carriage and tralala and frisky all belong to uncle hasan and that he himself is the driver. all the kids on the bosphorus know him and tralala and frisky, the second horse who pulls the carriage. because there aren't any other drivers on this side of the bosphorus who have their own buggy and carriage. he's one of a kind our uncle hasan.

you write,,, you keep going on and on,,, are these the things you really want to say,,, zeyyat will be here in a bit,,, your ex,,, and your husband is out there on the balcony,,, what are you saying,,, what do you expect, from all of this,,, look at the present,,, forget the past,,, look at the world,,, the world is on fire,,, look at your country,,, fathers and sons burying daughters alive,,, the act of burying they learned from a crow,,, "and then god sent a crow; it scratched at the ground to show him how to bury his brother! woe is me! he said; outdone by a crow, without enough sense to cover my brother's body! he then became one of the remorseful."

(surah al–maidah, 31)

tell about that girl,,, shovelfuls of rage mixed with earth,,, the father and son who buried her alive, the mother looking on from the window,,, had they taped her mouth shut,,, were there no neighbors around,,, could she not scream,,, did no one hear her,,, not even her mom?

***

the cold, chased into the corners of the sky by the early september quail storm, unleashes itself upon us come winter. my sister and i sleep in a cuddle yet despite the thick white wool sweaters aunt havva knit for us slivers of ice find our uncovered parts and gnaw at them, in the daytime the stove in the courtyard and the one on the middle floor burn but just barely,,, it's mostly the stove in the kitchen that warms us. uncle lights it every morning, the water boiling in the teapot and the steam rising from food warms the air, and then uncle lights the stove in the courtyard too. we're always hardly warm in winter. mother irons the sheets and blankets with red-hot bricks before putting us to bed, shivering we climb under the covers. here it's freezing cold in all the houses this time of year uncle tells us that nobody ever gets cold in africa. there the sun scorches you all year round he says...

i don't have a father,,, he died just before i was born,,, i hug my sister every chance i get,,, it's okay, she says, don't worry, we've got our mother and our aunt too,,, and our great-great-grandfather nobody can hurt us. which grandfather? you know, bigbeargramps!? the one who's our aunt's grandfather too; the one who never dies; in küçüksu,,, you mean the one who lets us use his oxcart for picnics? he could come to our rescue? of course he's really rich don't you know,,, he's got a big farm, and farmhands...

but i can't sleep,,, i'm scared,,, what is it that troubles me,,, i wake up early,,, my sister is asleep,,, my nose pressed against the tiny window of the attic i watch the day approaching,,, and how gog magog scurry sneakily along the wall carrying bizarre misshapen weights in their hands,,, i watch the pale red that the sea seeks to swallow as it changes color, time arriving in the form of silent waves, the pitch black darkness hiding deep beneath the green, galata tower wrapped in a lace of fog, still heavy with slumber. galata tower meanwhile eyes hagia sophia on the opposite shore. it stands tall but as soon as the pink of daylight touches the sea and snuffs out the darkness silently it wails, if only i were hagia sophia and you galata tower. then once the waves of time begin receding to the shores of my brain and fading away i curl up next to my sister and filled with worry about how hard it will be to unravel this complicated world i drift off to sleep.

***

i loved zeyyat but sabit and i were still flirting,,, he told me while we walked around sultanahmet that he was going to show me a nonreligious monument. something special, as almost all the others there were religious. this one isn't though, it's made of egyptian granite, and some say it was cleopatra who had it erected. look what's written on it:

> *only emperor theodosius dared to erect this four-sided column which had lain heavy on the earth, and so he charged proclus with the task, and machines erected this awe-inspiring mass in sixty days.*

not sixty days, thirty-two, he said.

i didn't know you were so interested in stones!

i'm interested in history not stones; here come look at what the inscription next to it says:

> *formerly it (was) difficult to obey noble masters (but) (i) was ordered to bear the wreath of victory over dead tyrants;*
> *all bow down to theodosius and his eternal off-spring*
> *thus in thirty-two days (i) was prevailed over, and in the time of praefectus proklos was (i) raised toward the skies.*

would you look at that, a talking stone! he said. first we laughed, and then i threw my arms around his neck and there in front of the obelisk of theodosius we kissed for the first time. what's come over you! he said, i have sooo many more stones to tell you about; i'm not about to let a kiss stop me!..

that day i thought i was in love with sabit not zeyyat.

***

i never understood how that woman was our aunt. her glasses never stayed put, always slid off her nose and fell to the floor, hand me my glasses twinkle-eyes. her home was a two-story villa on a plot of land behind küçüksu palace just past asaf's gazino. there she lived with her armenian daughter sultan whom she'd taken in as a baby and raised

sultan never knew she was armenian

she must be around 10 years old at this time

no matter where sultan is, whether close by my aunt, in the kitchen downstairs, or out weeding the garden

whenever auntie starts knitting a new row, without taking her eyes off her needles she yells out:

hey you little hussy what's running through that head of yours huh; don't make me come after you with my slipper!

auntie, sultan's downstairs in the kitchen, she can't hear you, my sister would say

oh yes she can, you bet she can, you have no idea how well she can hear; she's not downstairs she's standing on the steps listening to us, go see for yourself; i know, i can tell from the smell.

does sultan stink auntie? i'd ask

she does but only i can smell her

as time passed and the middle-aged inhabitants of fener grew old or descended underground and i made my way toward womanhood on my own i became obsessed with søren,,, yes, i know,,, i know what you're going to say, the father decided not to kill his son at the last minute, what more do you want,,, yet he didn't change his mind,,, religious texts always trick us like that,,, he never once changed his mind; he'd already vowed to follow god's commands as it were; if god—from wherever he sat, or stood, on high—had not rolled that ram down to abraham

wouldn't abraham have sacrificed isaac

without batting an eye?

we may as well call him isaac's murderer

whether isaac was born of sarah

or ishmael, of hagar

whichever

what difference does it make

some say it was ishmael he was going to kill

others say it was isaac

if you ask me i'd say isaac too

why i decided on isaac i can't say

isaac is made of sorrow

like me

yes, oh yes

of sorrow you say

why, I don't know

sallow-faced isaac

who never questions but obeys

only senses

isaac is made of child hues

but as for me, i question

"a man in samsun amasya was taken into custody for throwing his two children out the window while under the influence of a dream. the man, believed to have suffered an emotional breakdown, stated, i saw the prophet muhammad in a dream, he said to me, throw your children out the window (ap)."

***

the strange thing is that søren
has come down to us in the present day
alongside the west's greatest philosophers
by way of tradition
yet was it not
while seeking paths of liberation
from the burden
or perhaps the tyranny of tradition
that in the spring of youth
we found ourselves at protests
at protests, together
revolutionaries
united
by the sentiment "enough is enough"
on may 1st workers' day one year
in taksim
firm in our belief that humanity's sole salvation
lay in the victory of the proletariat
gathered in front of gezi park we shook heaven and earth

roaring our anthem, a brand-new sun shall rise

from the horizons of my homeland

thousands of voices in a single cry

to cast off tradition

squeezing into taksim square

packed together, shoulder to shoulder

this celebration is ours we thought

we are strong we thought

when from out of nowhere

bearded monks in potur pants

surrounded us clamoring, allahu akbaaar!

the koran in their hands

a brand-new sun in the sky

clutching divine clubs fresh from the lathe

waving radiant flags of jihad green

from the abrahamic realms they descended upon us

fists clubs kicks

as if to say: you asked for the dictatorship of the working class, you got it, take this!

we're stunned

blood drenches us

spilled by the violence of the ruthless pious

blood streams from my nose

şükran kurdakul who said the meaning of life

consists of living for the sake of others unconditionally

cups his teeth in his hand

in a flurry of mad punches

aydın hatipoğlu is beating the man who hit şükran

bekir yıldız

tussles with the plainclothes cops on his back

we made it this far by the star of our brow

you phony zealots

some people bolt past us

as for me, pushing my way through those thickets

greened by nettled brutishness

i came to

and all at once transformed my existence

into that of nemesis

bellowing, i'll show you

mid-swing i grabbed the club of the bearded man

who was clubbing me

and with the fossilized antlers of a wild deer

that i thrust forth from my nipples

i laid into that goon's stomach

so ferociously that he froze in fear

showing him what's what, i rubbed his cocky nose in the dirt

but then hearing allahu akbaaar

coming up from behind by the thousands

i fled as fast as i could

to the bathroom of the old park hotel

where we regathered, wondering whether to go back and fight

though it was plain as day our side had been routed

just two days earlier

at that same park hotel

quipping to our buddy edy, the plump hotel pianist

play something sam!

we sank into the lounge's velvet chairs, me and zeyyat

he with his philosophy that time and again societies like ours make intellectuals pay the price for the neuroses

brought on by societies' own backwardness

with the luster of green olives

cavorting at the bottom of martini glasses

our eyes locked, making love

at that park hotel which today

is but ashen enmity

between me and constantinople

he told me about his family that day zeyyat

how his father was kurdish

and his mother was from the town of havran

how in the basement of their home

in a workroomish space

they'd press oil from olives

delighting in the task

zeyyat lost himself in those olives

as if i weren't even there

in my head i was saying to him

stop babbling you fool, or i won't love you anymore

i couldn't care less about your damn olives

or where your parents came from

i fixed my gaze on a couple nuzzling at a table across the way

he didn't get it

it was olive this and olive that

how they changed color

the scent of the oil oozing out of them

in meticulous detail he described

every step in the transformation from tree to oil

you know, i really don't like olives, i said

he wavered

but,

what about the ones in martinis...

they're the only kind i like, i said

i've bored you, he said

reaching for his glass

if only you knew how adorable you are, i said

i took hold of his offended hand

he sighed in relief

***

i don't know why but i simply could not get kierkegaard out of my mind...

wasn't the root of "angst" the ego,,, that which protects us from anxiety. you know, those egos that made me myself and we ourselves when they were let loose from the cistern

or do you think that in fact i too am a kierkgaardian in pursuit of anxiety and truth,,, that damn truth! i mean essence,,, wait no, wasn't the essence of an object the object of experience? that thing called truth is driving me crazy! he says truth is that which we comprehend by making it part of our lives solely through our own sense of responsibility,,, that's what *he* says,,, i'm not about to give up pursuing my thoughts for no reason,,, what i'm up against here is a philosopher who is passionate about nothing but christianity,,, not only that, he must have gotten mixed up in his father's favored sect of pietism,,, just what exactly, my dear readers, has the world gained by dint of kierkegaard's reasoning of the abraham-isaac legend,,, that the dialectic of faith is the finest of all,,, the thoughts he expressed still cause pain today,,, this idée fixe exists in all orders and cults, in all hegemonic powers, from our aunt to those hogtying torturers...

but isn't the actual father, the father of fathers, st. augustine; pal of plato, that remnant of the 340s bc,,, the great philosopher of the west, st. augustine!,,, who also left his mark on islamic philosophy,,, in fact he was obsédé too just like our aunt you know, that aunt of mine who lived in küçüksu

the one who said she loved me and my sister so much

my father's little sister

who at every turn scared us out of our wits,,, reminding us we were going to burn in hell

never once letting us forget about crime and punishment

or the afterlife!

such that she'd often slip into my dreams,,, at night our aunt takes us for a ride,,, she drives the horses,,, having hitched frisky to the buggy herself,,, with a spirited neigh, frisky takes to the sky,,, in the darkness every strand of her flaxen mane a golden whip snaps in our faces,,, auntie bursts into laughter as she pulls the buggy to a halt,,, saying, well i told you two you were bound for infernal flames, she grabs us by the arms, flinging first my sister and then me into hell!

dear readers i don't know whose idea it was but they've laid my aunt to rest above all the cemetery entrances,,, she grinds her teeth at passersby proclaiming, you too shall taste death you too shall taste death, you cannot escape it, soon every single one of you too shall taste death...

***

ayda to moro mu

hayda to yavri mu

den ta tu to foreso ali mia

with the first warmth of spring

this song would rise up

into the sky of the new republic

through the upturned horns of gramophones

through speakers

from countryside picnic grounds

from the lands of greeks not yet driven away

from the princes' islands to the streets of moda

from caddebostan's maksim nightclub

to asaf's gazino in küçüksu

from the beach club of suadiye

to reşit bey beach in caddebostan...

that last beach, reşit bey beach in caddebostan

is across from the villa of our relatives where we'd sometimes stay for several days at a time, next to ragıp pasha mansion

we kids would sneak through ragıp pasha grove and onto the beach without buying tickets

from the mansion's marble-clad jetty we'd jump into the sea

catch our breath on a small outcropping a few hundred yards away

swim up to the beach

and sprawl out on the sand beside our mothers who did buy tickets

much later i'd find out

at the home of my first husband into whose arms i'd thrown myself
seeking to soothe that feeling of lack born of not having truly lived

(that was my husband before sabit, a marriage so brief that by now
you could say it never really happened)

it was while living with him

back when i became a bookworm that i learned about reşit bey

it was during that period of gloom i found out

reşit bey was a member of the turkish communist party

and while i lay on the sand

flirting with hayri

a tall fair-skinned communist youth

reşit bey was rotting away in jail

longing for the sun

as he cried out the sun, oh the sun! is it not for us that you exist

he was ripped from the courtyard

by the temporary sultans of the time

first his fingernails pulled out

then bastinadoed

together with his friends

reşit bey

if he's no longer living

may the earth in which he lies

be enveloped by the sparkling silky sand of his beach

may the waters of his sea

his suns reflected off the water

his moons

his stars

fall to his breast

along with so many others, some whose names we knew, some we didn't

killed before their time

may nature embrace them all in her bosom

back when fingerless hamdi's boys

were at their most vicious

but right now we don't know what kind of people they are, the owner of reşit bey beach and his friends

we're little so very very little

we don't know

why some people

suffer torture for others

why they're thrown from the windows

of sanasaryan han onto the street

in so-called "suicides"

***

my sister's face gleamed like a candy apple.

we were looking at the cistern where iris said ego was hiding,,, we'd stolen the key to the lid of the cistern from the cupboard where my mother hid it and opened it up. all the kids were there that day,,, children's heads hanging down over the edge of the cistern,,, inside it was the color of a pitch-dark coffin shroud,,, no wait,,, what we saw was dead water, timeless heavy aged, stretched taut like dark green canvas,,, iris leaned far out over the lip of the opening,,, say what you want but i heard from above that uncle is hiding ego there under the water, she said,,, we closed the lid,,, that was where i saw it, mesrop said, a shadow on the wall of the well, then my sister and the other kids, all of us fell silent. we looked at each other, children's faces floundering, never able to decide what to grab onto when grappling with feelings too heavy for the soul to bear

children's faces persistent in their search for ego yet indecisive in their stubbornness, aggrieved faces intertwined like pots of geraniums placed on the balconies of row houses along a city street

children's faces like rowboats in a slumberous embrace along the shores of the golden horn where vangel's mother said you'd find ingots upon ingots of gold if you dug into the seabed

impatient children's faces furtively watching petro-birds, swallows, barges girded with old car tires, the troubled faces of greek youths adorning the windows of the red greek school for boys, the small veteran ferries plying their routes...

uncle was always pleased when he saw those faces all gathered together

he'd open his maw:

"in the name of earthly order an article was thus appended to the sultanic code of law thenceforth legitimizing the murder of their brethren;

and so as soon as mehmed the conquerer became sultan

he had little six-month-old prince ahmed strangled

earringed selim poisoned his father bayezid II

and then

had five of his blood nephews executed

along with his brother prince korkut

and his brother prince ahmed

suleiman the magnificent

had piri reis put to death

forget about the people

this republic, which was pulled with forceps

from the vagina of the empire they called the east

still hasn't recovered

after all these years

sultan mehmed III had 101 siblings

upon ascending the throne he had oak coffins made

for his 19 surviving brothers

and ordered them all strangled at once

he spiked some of their severed heads above the palace gate

others he stuffed with straw and sent to their families"

you're writing,,, you keep going on and on,,, what's a bunch of sultans to you anyway you know these aren't the things you really want to say,,, but there's an impulse you cannot control which tells you all of it matters,,, an impulse that keeps you from getting to the heart of it,,, just what the heart of it is you do not know,,, but you will find it,,, enough already,,, can you find it by talking about it,,, try to forget,,, what,,, forget already about that unknown thing you are seeking,,, take your pills,,, look you're old now,,, you're a respectable married woman with children,,, respectable,,, what do you mean respectable,,, what respectability,,, respectable as a part of the established system,,, respectable in the land of the respectables who bury their daughters in holes dug by crows...

***

no, even though like me he defends the notion that truth lies in subjectivity i drive him away from my borders,,, who? kierkegaard, who else,,, i'd never let him in through the gate of my burnt heart,,, in any case i haven't even decided myself yet if truth lies in subjectivity,,,

and for now i can't give any promises about whether i'll be able to do so by the end of this book,,, we'll have to wait and see,,, seeing as the subjective has foisted change upon the objective and the objective has foisted change upon the subjective,,, it's really not easy,,, yes we can defend søren as someone who was trying to make the best of the world's fear of raging hellfires in those times; in a sense his love was harmless. he said "how does one become a good christian, that's always been my priority." in his day and age that was what it meant to be a good person. all the same while we can accept that he was one of the first to examine the concept of "anxiety" what's the point,,, can't the concept of anxiety change? if we characterize it now as the consequence of neural activities what difference is it going to make?

what's more, i ask you, didn't the holy koran, in which believers claim every state of the human psyche is inscribed and described, in other words didn't our prophet hand down to us before everyone else all the revealings and revelations on this matter? if "anxiety" came into existence along with mortal beings did allah skip over that, the greatest of humanity's afflictions, and place the concept solely in søren's hands?

my dear readers we should waste no time in finding the seeds of "angst" among the wise insights of the koran so that infidel known as kierkegaard doesn't make off with the honor of being the first...

what i'm saying is, did søren root his theory in scientific premises? no!

without casting off myth, religion, ideologies, matters of gender,

the family

all the aggregates of social power

without being purified of the filth of these tsunamis

is it possible for a philosopher to arrive at a genuine theory?

at the truth of reality

the reality of truth

his essence and own substance

it is said that søren's real concern

was unseating hegel

please tell me dear reader

how does a thinker

arrive

at the crown gate of being a thinker

how does a thinker

arrive

at wisdom

without first being purified

of feelings of animosity and envy

what kind of a poem

is a thinker

spine-chilling

as in

the moon never beams, without bringing me dreams

after all, søren did say, “i wrote the poetics of religion”... perhaps his prose is poetic in danish, who knows,,, i’ll leave that to the enthusiasts...

* * *

war has broken out! my mother says. but there are no guns or cannons, no bombs to be seen, neither infantry nor aviators, those progeny of icarus, no dark-skinned cavalry on their pegasuses, or those sharply starched, red-blooded lotharios of the navy

oh that reminds me¦ rosa, you know, my classmate, she's dating a naval officer, every saturday they meet next to the pole holding up the giant iş bank coin bank in taksim and from there go to orman pub which is close to where the french cultural center is now. "he takes my hand and i feel i might faint, from the pleasure of it," rosa says,,, and for some reason this word "pleasure" gives me chills too...

they haven't kissed yet but rosa expects they will any day now. she says the naval officer's setting me up with one of his friends,

a blonde one please, i told rosa,,, i'll tell vedat this week she said

we'll make a splendid quartet we'll have loads of fun, vedat says

so i'm waiting for my handsome naval officer my heart beating fast eager to be on the verge of fainting myself when he takes my hand next to the iş bank coin bank. but that weekend, at their usual meeting spot next to the coin bank pole, rosa's left standing.

the naval officer doesn't show up,,, rosa waits for hours but he doesn't come,,, tears streaming down her face "it's because he's afraid" she keeps saying, "he left me because he's afraid; because i'm jewish! why else, he was in love with me!.."

when my time came to fall in love, at first my lovers and i would go to the meyhanes along the bosphorus, later we started going to çiçek pasajı in beyoğlu, where we became friends with the greek waiters—until certain people drove them out of these lands, that is—who would cry out "hey bartender, send some arjantin pints this way," and greet us, "thoristo pasam... endoxi..." and later "a fahrettin kerim for pasam."

– zeyyat, there's something i want to tell you

– tell me my rose

– i want you to decorate my coffin when i die

– now where did that come from

– i don't want that green cover; you know those purple caftans with the silver embroidery; that's what i want on my coffin

– ...

– you hear me

– ...

– i do but i don't understand why you're thinking of death right now,,, are you trying to be funny? besides, that thing wouldn't cover an entire coffin, it's too short!

– you can use a different color to cover the parts where it's too short

– as you wish darling! which color!

– could be blue, or red, whichever color you like!

– how about blue; the color of emil galip's coffin!

– oh, now that would be wonderful, emil's color...

– how do you know you're going to die before me

– i don't, but if I do...

– why? i'm older than you

– doesn't matter, i can't ask my husband for something like this

– why not?

– he wouldn't take me seriously, and besides, i don't trust him,,, he'd just say, what does it matter if it's green or white or any other color, you'll be dead anyway

– why on earth bring this up now; i don't like you talking this way; how can you think of death at our warmest moment

– i don't know, i'm terrified of dying; besides, i think i'm in love with you

– and i with you,,, but dying is the last thing on my mind while we're making love, or even after. if we die, we die, and we'll be together till we do.

– hold me.

– maybe we can tell sabit one day

– tell him what?

– that we're in love, that he needs to leave you, he's a civilized man, he'll understand

– oh no don't you dare he wouldn't understand! he wouldn't understand, zeyyat! you don't know him

– i can convince him, he loves me, i'll tell him it's simply human, that you and i are in love; he'll understand...

– oh no don't you dare do something like that...

– but you told me he has a lover himself, maybe getting a divorce would make things easier for him too

– no it wouldn't! he's a coward, don't you know that,,, sabit and changing the order of things? no way! if you so much as put his teacup in a different spot than usual his entire life would be turned upside down, he'd probably go and try to kill himself again or something; you know that

– alright alright don't get upset,,, so what are we going to do about this. the truth is i really don't like cheating on my best friend with his wife!?..

– how about some music, mozart?

– noooo, schubert lieder!...

– we need to do something, this is wrong...

– there's nothing we can do!

– enough already! come on, get up, let's have a smoke, why did you have to go and bring all this up again! cognac?

– that'd be lovely

– alright but don't get dressed just put on the caftan, i'll be right back.

***

what of when he said "the dialectic of faith is the most refined and most remarkable of all..."?,,, you too my dear readers should think carefully before answering,,, because søren also says:

"...regardless, if that's what he commanded, he was prepared to sacrifice him. his belief was steeped in the grace of absurdity, after all, human reckoning is undoubtedly infallible, and the fact that the god who ordered abraham to kill isaac annulled his injunction mere moments later truly was absurd. abraham climbed the mountain. even as the knife gleamed in his hand he believed... god would not give the command for isaac..."

so there you have it, "the grace of absurdity!" certain that god wouldn't give the order yet with his "at your command" servility, abraham was all set to butcher his son!..

at this point let's burst into a terrifying guffaw like uncle then keep going:

and please dear readers let's think about marx. oh come on he's outdated you say, as a cognitive "new subject" let's turn your thoughts to adorno, foucault,,, to bakhtin,,, to bakhtin,,, when bakhtin says, "carnival brings together, unifies, weds, and combines the sacred with the profane, the lofty with the low, the great with the insignificant, the wise with the stupid..." what exactly does he mean? but my true foundation is wittgenstein! he's on my side, when he says "wisdom is passionless." as do i! and what about j.-p. sartre? that atheist thinker, why did he heap such praise on søren,,, would today's world of thought really be any worse off without søren's ideas?

so you say,,, but the construction of the world of thought as a whole, is it any different from the construction of history,,, yet here you are trying to pull a brick out of that edifice,,, still, ishmael and isaac, their father really did it, he went off and killed them both,,,

the dialectic of faith, ha!

is "the dialectic of faith" god? is it faithlessness? the grace of absurdity? the absurdity of grace?

***

it was a lot of work but at last we got the blackout curtains hung up; opaque roller blinds made from dark blue oilcloth, the kind that pull down and reel back up, spring-loaded pulleys at the top: "don't be scared, those bastards' airplanes are flying blind up there. they can't do a thing to us!" mother says while washing the dishes in the basement, followed by: "*...like all loves will this too come to an end, i wonder...*" yet again she's enraptured, singing and dancing with uncle,,, one of her red suede farandole shoes tapping out the rhythm on the maltese limestone floor,,, dishpan on the counter, she hands us the dishes she's washed and rinsed,,, we dry them off, my sister and i, and put them away,,, humming, she cheerfully makes her way upstairs

> *you fled like a seagull longing for distant coasts*
> *far from the shores of my heart, from the horizon of my eyes...*

make me a strong cup of coffee, she says, i think i'll have a smoke too, but just then the flash of a mirror from one of the houses across the way flickers across her face,,, mother exclaims, "they're holding up a mirror! that's a very bad thing to do, my little darlings, don't let your uncle hear about this" and for a long time the blackout curtains are kept closed, even during the day...

***

these are the times when we sweeten our tea with raisins; get our bread with ration cards; aunt havva's son sabahattin walks the neighborhood from dawn till dusk trying to sell newspapers, *sabah, akşam, tercüman, cumhuriyet, vatan,* which he carries in a satchel slung around his neck,,, uncle reads every single column by vâlâ nurettin and mother reads *readers digest,* though a copy of the book *letters from my windmill* never leaves her bedside table and never will for as long as she lives... sabahattin's mother sews clothes for us on our hand-crank singer sewing machine, my sister reads nâzım hikmet's poems to me from the onionskin copies she can get her hands on: whatever you do, don't tell anyone, his poetry's been banned,,, when evening falls and we go up to the attic, she takes out those pink onionskin sheets of paper and reads to me for hours on end,,, i don't understand a thing,,, these poems are going to save people, she says,,, how, i ask,,, you'll see, she says,,, "the rowboat rises / the rowboat falls," that's all that sticks in my mind... and from there to the rowboats of the ferrymen crossing the golden horn from fener to karaköy,,, then we're in göksu rowing to dört kardeşler in the boat of a fisherman my aunt knew; grasping the slippery round handle of the right-side oar with both hands i couldn't be happier,,, my sister pulls at the oar on the left,,, it's our first time rowing,,, the fisherman, he's at the rudder; he keeps calling out, "dip your oars in the sea!",,, dip your oars, not that much, let up a little, just below the surface, not so deep now, nothing to be scared of, puulll!..

you're still writing,,, you're a married woman now, settled down,,, getting on in years,,, your husband is out on the balcony puffing on his cigar,,, newspaper in hand,,, le monde,,, but soon that man will be here, your former lover, current confidante, or should you say friend, you're not sure what to call him,,, zeyyat,,, you and he were once laden with a freight of feelings for one another,,, you know, that same "friend" you held hands with while watching tarkovsky movies back in the day,,, who you often met up with at the park hotel,,, where he'd quip to edy, "play something sam",,, he's on his way now...

***

uncle said,

i hacked off isaac's head, see, just like your mother's fatwa commanded!

then he broke out in one of his rabid laughs

over isaac's dead body

and without even the slightest limp lifted isaac off the ground

as we made our way up the stairs

his chalky face expressionless

like kaidanovsky in tarkovsky's stalker

he was plucking isaac

his eyes never leaving us

let's kill him, my sister said

how i asked

we can poison him she said

okay i said

but we knew nothing about poison

or killing people

nor had we seen tarkovsky's kaidanovsky yet

we were little, so very very little...

"stop the disappearances
prosecute the perpetrators"
reads the passing picket sign,,, ferhat tepe
disappeared under custody. his tortured body
found in lake hazar. the charges
dismissed,,, musa anter,,,
vedat aydın,,, yılmaz demir,
in his righteous struggle our honor resides
fikri sönmez, sinan suner,
yaşar sucu, his heart bursting
with love for humanity, ahmet uzun,
alaattin demirci,
kenan şengöz, hatice özen
her eyes forever smiling
kenan budak, president of
the progressive leatherworkers' union,
mehmet sözer,
known for his valor in captivity...
"prosecute the perpetrators..."

zeyyat will be here in a little bit,,, he who once told you not to marry sabit,,, my lover, the lines of his hands so like the lines of my own, "don't do it, you won't be happy with him",,, who, in his letters to you after you broke up following those words, tried to tell you that he himself was your truth,,, he doesn't know you still keep all his letters,,, in a locked drawer

* * *

i keep saying it was the prophet abraham who killed isaac begat of sarah,,, and ishmael begat of hagar too,,, was this prophet abraham not the same father who thrust the first religion of the book into our world?.. what difference would it make if he'd only killed ishmael begat of hagar,,, the brain obsesses over it,,, the question claws at the mind,,, insistent,,, the torah mentions it several times,,, which son he killed,,, but that's irrelevant,,, what i'm telling you is that a father butchered his son because god asked him to,,, from there the memory leaps to the tale of the shepherd with pierced feet,,, then to the "oedipus complex",,, to patricide,,, a look back back at tribes who butchered daughters at birth gorging themselves on a family feast,,, the torments of humanity en route to our present civilization laid bare...

back then, uncle's still alive. raggedy mefkûre's father, ferit, pulls at the shrunken sleeves of his old jacket whenever he speaks,,, a wide-eyed oddball with a face covered in cracks like an aged oil painting,,, the whole neighborhood makes fun of him,,, he's always going on about how ego removed a bullet from flesh, how it helped mares through painless births, stuff like that,,, always repeating the same words again and again. sometimes we'd ask him why he kept saying the same thing over and over and he'd answer, palilalia palilalia palilalia,,, "ego removed a bullet from my thigh, ego removed a bullet from my thigh, ego removed a bullet from my thigh..." he was the butt of everyone's jokes,,, we'd ask uncle if what ferit said was true, "it's true, absolutely true, the police mistook him for a burglar and shot him. you can't assume someone's a liar just because they repeat themselves, people who say things only once are more likely to be lying" ...there was no reason for us to believe uncle but in our neighborhood he carried a certain clout,,, that's why everyone came to believe that he and ego were more or less thick as thieves. "ego has such magical hands,,," he ran his eyes over his own huge hands with their coarse nails,,, they could midwife mares through painless births,,, ego could very well be a sea creature that emerged from the golden horn of mixed blood descended from two fathers he'd add laughing inwardly, gleeful at the sight of our confusion...

at times like this my mother would break out in violent laughter, guffawing in uncle's face,,, she'd turn into a kallikantzaros about to board one of auntie's djinn carriages,,, stare silently at the ceiling for a while,,, then as if nothing had happened, with a tense smile on her face she'd begin

kamer çehre peri-ru / tende canım
nigarım, dilberim, ruh-i revanım
enisim, sim-berim yar-i vefadarım...

she sang this song in a deep baritone voice that couldn't possibly be coming from her,,, and it was the only alaturka song my mother knew; "it's actually my mom's song," she'd say. to those who asked how she could muster such a mannish voice "it isn't mine," she'd say, "it's just like my mom's, takes over my vocal chords as soon as i start singing this song, i don't get it either!"

on october 9, 1978, three armed men walked up to an apartment where two hacettepe university students were living. but that night several other students were there too. in the apartment that night were serdar alten, hürcan gürses, efraim ezgin, latif can, osman nuri uzunlar, faruk ersan, and salih gevenci.

in his deposition to the ankara martial law prosecutor's office, haluk kırcı said as follows: "we knocked on the door and as soon as it opened we went in and made them all lie down on the floor. we sent one of our guys out to the big boss, abdullah (çatlı), to get orders for what to do next. abdullah sent over some cotton and ether, telling us to knock them unconscious and kill them one by one. next i went out to the car to speak with abdullah myself. i told him it was going to be hard to kill them inside the apartment, and suggested we take them away two at a time and kill them somewhere else. he said 'okay.' so we put two of them in his car and took them out to the eskişehir highway. once we found a suitable spot we had them lie down on the ground, and then we shot both of them in the head. after that we went back to the apartment. realizing it would be hard to get the job done like this too, abdullah said we should strangle them one at a time instead. i managed to strangle one. but it was going to be hard to kill the rest like that. so i sent our guys away and proceeded to empty my clip into the four of them sitting on the sofa, shooting them at close range. then i took the gun to abdullah." one of the four revolutionaries lying on the floor, serdar alten, was still alive but just barely. in the statement he gave before he died, he said that the men who murdered his friends were pro-mhp fascists. they were abdullah çatlı, ibrahim çiftçi, and haluk kırcı.

***

the house is at the top of the hill. when you go down and turn left—the hills in fener are strewn with steep, winding alleys—keep going then veer right, in a few hundred yards we arrive at the patriarchate, where my sister sometimes lights votives; i look up at the two corinthian columns of the doors of the lodging annex, the date 1500 visible above them. the "patrikaekhiki astiki skoli maraslı" the elementary school with its attached facade, funded by the russian orthodox grigorios maraslis who, it was so imagined, would one day save the greeks from the wrath of the turks; some nights i wander on its roof like a somnambulist casting dreams upon myself whenever isaac's shadow falls on my curtain,,, i dash to the rooftop window,,, in that solitude on the blackening teal roof of skoli maraslı our rowboat departs from a little bay filled with tiny vessels of light that float blinking in the dark,,, my sister, efthim, me, vangel, and the cool air; by then we've poisoned uncle and buried him in eyüp sultan,,, nudged along by the rhythm of a gentle barcaruola our gondola slips across the silvery cinder seas of the night, two couples,,, we embrace "as dusk falls over the opposite shore / where the sun's light wanes night in and night out..."

as the song nears its end the waves of the bosphorus begin tossing us about,,, the rowboat rises, the rowboat falls,,, gliding over the frothing waves it moors in front of the coffeehouse frequented by men under the wooden bridge where göksu creek meets the bosphorus,,, a little farther away uncle hasan's buggy awaits,,, we get out of the boat and walk through the ruins of the fortress, which have crumbled all the way down to the sea, and make our way to that place called toplarönu breaking into giggles, and dive into the clear waters of the bosphorus,,, i'm doing backstrokes,,, as is vangel,,, his curls turn a darker shade in the water,,, the sun! which herakleitos said "is new each day" dips its rays into the indigo sea,,, my sister and efthim are kissing in the sea,,, me, the water, the sun, and vangel,,, we are in love,,, our eyes deepening wells as we gaze at each other,,, i dive down to the bottom vangel follows, his chest brushing against my leg,,, hand in hand we emerge back into the sunlight, gasping for breath,,, i can't tell if i'm embarrassed or scared,,, the feeling hides inside my cheeks,,, then, out of nowhere, isaac!,,, isaac's crest atop vangel's head,,, flaming red,,, is it he who's with me,,, or isaac,,, his crest touches me,,, take a deep breath,,, dive into the depths,,, vangel's left behind,,, he's not coming,,, sunlight again,,, take another breath,,, go down then come back up,,, forget about isaac,,, forget about uncle,,, remember rosa, that resounding "crack",,, up-down, the far end, the entry and exit,,, rosa,,, the garden,,, are there any letters for me,,, no,,, that's a lie,,, uncle's hiding my letters,,, dive down,,, surface again,,, the garden gate, the border beyond,,, at night gog magog spy on us through the window, tree-trunk torso, head of a crab, barbed suckers pressed against the glass,,, i wake up in a fright,,, shanties have cropped up all along the garden walls,,, so many gog magogs now,,, they're multiplying,,, leave them be poor things, let them stay,,, my mother says,,, it's the right thing to do,,, they don't know right from wrong, uncle grunts, you'll see what they'll get up to in the end,,, "you've swum out too far, you'll be swept up by the current, your sister's gotten out already,,," then mother stands up and calls to us,,, wearing a dusk-colored handknit swimsuit she gets up from where she's been sunbathing, raises one hand to her forehead to shield her eyes from the sun,,, come out quickly now,,, then she disappears and auntie comes to pick us up, we get in the buggy,,, a bay horse,,, my tralala,,, fixes her eyes of coal on me, whinnying with laughter as always,,, i respond with a grin,,, take us to dört kardeşler auntie says to uncle hasan the coachman,,, as for you two, you're going to get burnt to a crisp in the flames of hell, flaunting your bodies like that in front of strangers,,, my sister says, but your legs are always bare, you never wear stockings,,, that doesn't count, auntie replies, god knows full well why i don't wear them,,, but why, auntie, won't you tell us please, my sister says,,, because they burn my legs,,, make them all itchy,,, so don't wear stockings, no harm in that, my sister says, men have legs too and it's not a sin for them, she adds,,, that's another story, but in any case they give me sores,,, then i get sick, auntie says,,, why is god so mean to you, i ask,,, zip it, she says, knee-high twerps like you ought to keep your nose out of grown-ups' business... tralala starts sneezing,,, and at the same time farting and making scuffling sounds,,, auntie says to uncle hasan, what on earth did you feed her,,, this time around,,, tralala gently ambles forward,,, turning to us, uncle hasan says, i had a hard enough time just getting her hitched to the buggy this morning, and then he lightly flicks her haunches with his whip,,, i'm going to go to bed now, my sister says, and all the while i'm rambling on to her about my dreams; mother, "girls! lights out!",,, what did you wish for when you lit a candle at the church today? i ask my sister, "i'm not telling you," she says, "if i do, it won't come true"...

a young man holds a photograph,,, beneath the photograph: "faruk eren, disappeared in police custody on the 21st of november 1980; one of the first disappearances that year",,, emine ocak holds a photograph of her son hasan ocak, "i'm looking for a grave to cover in flowers!" mother ocak says,,, the specters of thousands of young men most of them kurdish haunt the living,,, the bodies of the dead are nowhere to be found... it's just like when rosa luxemburg was disappeared in berlin in 1919. years later it became clear that the headless footless handless corpse kept in the anatomy depot at berlin's charité hospital belonged to r.luxemburg. according to the nazis this method was much more effective, much more persuasive than public killings and executions...

***

mother:

– i cooked isaac, take him to havva so she can feed him to sabahattin

– no! we won't give him to her! my sister said

– me neither! i said

she took me into her arms. sabahattin, he's got tuberculosis, poor thing, he'll die if he doesn't get some decent food into him, that's the whole reason we killed isaac

– we're not gonna take him, so there! my sister said

– i'm not gonna either, so there! i said

– fine, i'll do it myself, mother said

nothing ever dies, not isaac nor anything else, they change dimension that's all, they'll never be forgotten she went on to say,,, god created singing and dancing so we can forget the bad things that happen she said,,, song and dance make us beautiful on the inside,,, would dancing make isaac happy i said,,, it would, she said, song and dance make the dead happy, through songs the past and future become one, they're brought to life,,, and what about father would they bring him to life too,,, the minute hand of her face stopped,,, yes, him too! she said,,, she hugged me tightly, gave me a big kiss, set me down, then turning to my sister said, come on you join in too, a-one a-two, a-one-two-three go! with our right feet we stomped on the marble floor; the moment the three of us started doing the farandole, poised regally as royalty, uncle was out the door.

a bloody cock's crest stirred inside me for years,,, my sister and i went into gog magog's shack,,, they'd had a lot of kids,,, done up the place,,, uncle slaughtered isaac, we said, and you're yajuj majuj, that's what he told us, we said,,, they didn't say a word, i grabbed hold of magog's gnarled trunk, who is uncle really, tell me,,, we're going to kill him, i said,,, magog was shorter and thinner than gog,,, he shrugged off my hand,,, the tongue they spoke was sealed off to us, their mannerisms evoked no meaning, a guttural vernacular we did not understand,,, uncle calls you "hınkır mınkır" i said,,, and he shouts "vagina data, vagina data!" in the middle of the night, my sister said. baldy caught my skirt in his mouth and started pulling at it... oh damn, hang on a sec; it's time for my pills again!..

when i had an operation on my gallbladder last year, i joked to the doctor that he should set aside the stones he removed because if they turned out to be jewels, i could sell them if i ever fell on hard times,,, i wondered if they'd find the pebbles of mosaics inside me, as i'd certainly breathed in my fair share of mosaic dust over the years,,, don't you worry about that, we show our patients everything we remove from them, the doctor said. this doctor was one of those somber types, not a humorous bone in his body but perfectly skilled with his hands. when i came to after the operation he said, i'm not sure how to tell you this but what we took out was rather bizarre,,, what do you mean, i asked,,, we couldn't tell what it was, this oddly shaped thing red like a poppy flower not something we could keep! maybe it was a piece of red coral! i suggested. he still didn't laugh, no, it was the color of a cock's crest, he said, soft and crumbly to the touch, and left.

***

one day when school was on break, when our almanac calendar announced the "start of the canicular season," and the carnivals of arnavutköy, üsküdar, and göksu had gotten underway

my dance partner vangel

came up to me and said

who're you going to marry when you grow up

you of course, i said

okay in that case let's dance...

efthim,

the same boy whose voice was wrapped in that letter, you know, "*yirise se perimeno yirise...*," whenever they went out for recess at the fener greek high school for boys

aunt lefkothea's son

nevin

şeref's partner

musa

partnering up with raggedy mefkûre

or whoever else happened to be there that day,

mesrop

with prying eyes he watches on from a distance

one of his legs was longer

or the other shorter

as for sabahattin he was never there

he'd be roaming the streets

of constantinople

calling out

read all about it, get your *akşam*, i've got *akşam, cumhuriyet, vatan, yeni sabah, tercüman...*

from çarşamba he'd walk to sirkeci

to eminönü, cağaloğlu, and balat

while resting by the ruins of tekfur palace

he'd make a meal of bread and olives

the bottoms of his shoes facing out

from the palace toward the sea

soles upon soles tacked into place by cobbler talip

but the years they changed soles too

as seen on the patched outsoles of comrade dink

lying facedown in front of *agos*

soles not of leather but of rubber

seared onto the emblem of our country

school of toothless cynics, with hot pitch

so who killed hrant you ask

well that remains a mystery

whoever killed

yaşar gündoğdu

sevinç özgüner

onat kutlar

mumcu

doğan öz

orhan keskin

necmettin büyükkaya

ibrahim kaypakkaya

and thousands more, that's who

for a while rosa had been irfan's girl,

then after high school she up and left for israel

i'll write you, she'd said

and i'm certain she did

but uncle hid the letters away, i'm sure of it...

once we've killed him we'll go into that room he keeps locked

break the latch with the same hammer i used to smash the pebble mosaics

and find rosa's letters, and uncle's grisly secret too.

if tayfun, yorgi, and efterpi also showed up

if they too came around on the same day to dance

we'd hold hands and make a circle

and if my mother didn't set up the gramophone we'd sing as we danced,

but if she did

the music and dance combined would sweep us clear off our feet

and it no longer mattered who partnered with whom

sounds,

beats,

volutions,

pausations,

leaping forward and drawing closer, a symmetry of glances

in the courtyard creating

sexual signals

that the future holds in store

in dance we fashion

anew

the farandole

an inner circle, an outer circle

spinning in opposite directions

the farandole

we skimmed from my mother's existence

my mother

who in search of a cure for the brevity of life

in the summeriest reaches of the day

craned back her luminous neck

and in each angle of her vanity mirror

turned left and right, examining her face

which she'd washed with puro soap

so fragrant and lathery

straight out of the "your skin is not laundry" ad

then dusted her powder puff, which resembled a tuft of birds disappearing into the horizon, with tokalon powder

blew lightly on the puff

closed her eyes and, moving upward from her neck, patted at her skin, cloaking her face in a pure white

deathly pallor

made a bow of her lips with fez-colored fox-brand lipstick

applied kohl,

freshened up her dark blonde curls

using a pair of coal tongs

then after slipping into the red frilled skirt she wore day in and day out pulled on a homeros-hued blouse, low-cut and collarless,

so tight it squeezed her breasts up like a bra,

her face of which we were besotted lovers captivating our gaze

she said to us "any woman can be as beautiful as venus, don't you ever forget that"

and now with her willowy arms she'll set up the gramophone

she'll place the tip of her shoe on the lid of the cistern where the egos are hiding, there in the marble-paved courtyard we call the "dance floor",,,

she'll lower her eyelids

wait until the rising and falling of her chest matches the rhythm of her heartbeat and then with a tip-tippy-tap tap-tap-tap on the cistern

she'll send word

and when the order comes from the egos in the cistern

she'll open her eyes

gingerly walk forward, piercing through our circle making her way to the very center

where she'll get caught up in the electricity of movements of her own invention, the songs, notes, rhythms surging through her lithe body drawing us into an ecstasy we didn't understand, arms hands, legs hips in wild motion, when suddenly she'd be stricken by one of her migraines; unable to bear it, covering her eyes with the crook of her arm she'd dash upstairs and collapse on her bed. yet now how easy it is to cure a migraine: boil some flat-leaf lady's mantle in a cup of water for twelve minutes, drink this brew warm once or twice a day, and that pesky affliction known as a migraine will be a thing of the past dear readers

back then aunt lefkothea used to take my mother to a saint that people called "yavedut sultan," it was actually a column in the church of hagia sophia known as "the sweating column"; a stone pillar that would sweat year-round no matter what the season. he was supposedly buried beneath it, that "sultan yavedut," who sweated nonstop when he was alive. and so you see whenever my mother rubbed that column's sweat on herself, she wouldn't get another migraine for months...

aunt lefkothea and her husband once took my mother and uncle to the tepebaşı gazino for a nikos gounaris and sofia vembo concert,,, the same night that efthim and vangel came round to our place, and what a night it was. vangel kissed me for the first time and efthim kissed my sister for the who knows how manyth time... for days afterward, my mother and uncle couldn't stop talking about the songs, costumes, and makeup of vedette chanteuse and vedette chanteur,,, but most of all they raved about that "fire-eating man duo harry" and the concert of another vedette chanteuse, maria vincent!..

uncle often impersonated duo harry for us, opened his mouth real wide this one time as if swallowing fire and dropped flat to the floor with a thud,,, cracked his head open,,, we stared down overjoyed at the thought of him dying right there on the spot,,, shaking it off, he got to his feet don't worry i'm fine, he said, it'd take a lot more than that to kill me!

you're writing, you keep going on and on,,, come back to the present,,, your husband's sitting right there,,, you've put some butter in a hammered copper skillet that once belonged to your mother,,, you're melting it,,, you're going to make semolina halva,,, the truth is here in this skillet you see,,, in the present,,, forget the past / you have no past,,, your truth is here in this kitchen,,, you, sabit, and zeyyat...

***

whenever we set out to breathe in the fragrance of life in beyoğlu, a life more opulent than that in fener, and gaze at the fancy storefronts and elegant apartment buildings that look nothing like our own houses, my mother transforms herself into the iridescent, striped, tasseled train of a peacock. everyone who sees her turns to take a second look. she has aunt havva sew her an imprimée dress each spring; "imprimée is a woman's second skin" she tells us; "any woman worth her salt owns a musk-scented imprimée embellished with buds and blossoms!"

first we go into lyon,,, the store across from the church of st. antoine.

this church is the glorious edifice described in ilhan berk's "the pigeons of st. antoine" and also in a short story by leylâ erbil in which a woman quarreling with a lover yells "piss off you geriatric creep!" its walls are the same color as my mother's blouse, a shade of rose, the setting sun.

at the entrance to the courtyard in front of the iron gates a romani woman sells evil eye charms and a black-bearded kurdish man hawks prayer beads. it isn't until later in life that ilhan berk sees istanbul for the first time; when he arrives here lahzen is in her twenties. she and one of her new lovers have lit a votive candle, asking jesus to reunite them soon. as lahzen and her lover walk down the marble stairs of the church into the courtyard, that slender arc—ilhan berk—glides past the kurdish prayer bead seller into the courtyard too,,, hands inside the pockets of his striped corduroy pants, olive drab.

he stops short right in front of lahzen and looks at her as if he doesn't know her then turns his head to the sky, but in truth he does know her and will meet her at the exact same spot the next day. he looks up at the sky as though seeing it for the first time before gliding through the open wing of the church's magnificent door.

when they meet up the next day and he says "you mean that was you lahzen!" oh how they laugh... "you'd like to make all the young fools fall in love with you, well let's see you try your magic on me!.." he says...

my mother's walked into the lyon store,,, how wonderful that she knows nothing about søren... how wonderful to live without knowing anything,,, in order to be truly oneself then, should one learn nothing at all,,, to grow up in a village in the middle of nowhere,,, to never know the city, be born in that village and die there,,, who knows how wonderful that must be,,, an empty unmoored rowboat adrift at sea,,, my mother's just a woman who loves the farandole,,, a self-contained being perhaps,,,

she's donned one of the black short-rimmed madame hats, amid shelves full of stacked bolts of fabric in a rainbow of colors towering all the way up to the ceiling, the pale young clerk who looks a lot like sabahattin and has dozed off under a 25-watt lamp springs to life at the sight of my mother. she's wearing the beige linen gloves sewn for her by auntie havva, to hide the nails she's bitten down to the quick... she points to the topmost shelf, "could you get that nile-blue and red one down for me please," no not that one the other one no the one next to it she says having the clerk bring down dozens of bolts one *thud!* after the other *thud!*. she wraps the fabric around herself and turns this way and that, admiring her reflection in the full-length mirror,,, without saying a thing she looks at the clerk as if asking something without asking anything at all,,, and he in return, it suits you very well my dear madam,,, but do take a look at this one too,,, and this one,,, and this one, why everything looks so good on you my dear madam, but this one here is simply marvelous,,, oh but then there's this,,, or how about this one,,, and so the haggling begins,,, at long last she tells him, that first roll you brought down,,, and so at a bargain price she gets a cut of three yards of imprimée! and cradling it in her arms as if it's an attic red-figure bowl she's afraid of dropping she steps out of the store, her face more beautiful than ever,,, as we make our way to the aznavur arcade, havva's going to sew you matching red muslin dresses for the next bairam, she says, you'll twinkle like little stars heh?.. when she's having a good day like this she speaks with an "heh!",,, i don't want to wear matching clothes with lahzen anymore, my sister says, she's still so little but i'm grown up now mom! then you pick whatever you like sweetheart; of course you have, you've grown so much, she says. and i get scared, thinking that it's just me all alone who's little now, i was little so very very little, there was no way i could know back then that mother flirted with men nor did i know the first thing yet about attic red-figure; i have no idea when i learned about all of this my dear readers. sometimes i think i'm some kind of magical being!; one of the enchanted, the accursed of this earth perhaps,,, actually no attic vases are pretty much the only interesting thing i know about,,, what's more i'm sick,,, not that i seem sick to myself,,, but since everyone else says so,,, truth is, i'm just tired,,, i should take my pills again and rest now my dear readers,,, the doctor said,,, don't worry it's nothing serious,,, with a little help you'll feel much better,,, but i didn't not one bit, still at our consultation i tell him yes you were right, i feel so much better now,,, sometimes i tell such lies to avoid upsetting the other person,,, in fact i think i've spent my entire life putting other people's feelings first,,, it's yet another symptom of my ailment,,, and so the doctor's quick to believe i'm getting better,,, keep it up he says warmly, you'll be right as rain in no time,,, but he's just a kid,,, what could you possibly understand about people at your age,,,

especially about women i mutter to myself,,, we shake hands,,, he walks his patient to the door,,, satisfied on the sly i leave, wondering on the way home if the little vermin would go around saying, "i've got this patient, she's a real nutcase",,, he's coiffed his reddish hair into a spiky pile on top of his head,,, had the sides shaved,,, ears jutting out,,, a pop star perhaps,,, god forbid he's one of those guys with fake credentials...

***

the european arcade, which an armenian named ohing had the italian architect pulgher design in pera in 1874, is in the neo-renaissance style.

aunt lefkothea calls it the "oyropeen arcade"

get me three yards of white "thassel" fringe while you're there won't you şehnaz i'm putting the money for it here

i'll pick up the change later

the mirrored arcade is full of small shops selling buttons and thread, girls sitting across from each other spinning silk on spindles.

mother and i are going to make our way to bogos's shop at number 18, but first she'll have a chat with yarn seller siranuş sarıcıyan,,, and in this way kind of teach us about our future lives.

siranuş must be around my age at the time

of all the napping heads on the counter we can't tell which belongs to siranuş and which to the cats

siranuş's father is garbis sarıcıyan whom my mother speaks of the same way she speaks of atatürk: if it weren't for atatürk, forget about coming this far, we couldn't so much as poke our noses out of our cages, slaves to men, that's what we were, always! but still girls you've got to be careful

protect yourselves from men

string them along but never give them the time of day.

each button made by garbis is a jewel my little darlings, each as valuable as a diamond brooch! here put one on your collar!

i've put two aside and got them fitted with pins, one for each of you, once you grow up a little they're yours; master garbis, he's a timeless artist,,, pursing her butterfly lips she speaks to siranuş. "master garbis is at lunch you say? give him my best, won't you, tell him şehnaz hanım from fener stopped by, he'll know..." whenever we come to this part of the city she shows to us this other woman she keeps alive inside herself, but we can't figure out who it is perhaps that vedette sofia vembo she can't stop carrying on about, but now we're so little so very very little we can't possibly wrap our minds around her, our mother...

you grew up, became a full-fledged woman,,, left all those small sorrows behind. you call them small now, yet the pain they caused you was anything but,,, boy did you give them a licking though,,, for years you grappled with the amorphous state of that pessimism you hadn't even noticed before, of existence transformed into sociality, until eventually within that magma existence was revived.

you and zeyyat will look at each other today as if the past never happened,,, your husband's best friend,,, they were classmates,,, sabit introduced you to zeyyat before you and sabit got married,,, my oldest friend, the one i told you about, he said,,, back then you thought you were in love with sabit,,, you'd kissed in the hippodrome,,, sabit's a good guy,,, never makes a fuss about your ex-lover,,, and he knows about the rest of them too,,, when zeyyat was in prison, the two of you used to visit him together,,, it made zeyyat so happy,,, would you look at that, my nearest and dearest are here to see me,,, he was always in good spirits,,, you never heard him complain about anything,,, only reminding us to bring him lemons,,, he was always asking for lemons,,, for years the two of you toted lemons to the prison,,, what do you do with them,,, they're for cleaning, he'd say,,, to kill off bacteria...

***

garbis usta works in madder paint or bone-colored paint on amber, those buttons of his adorned with swallows are famous among the denizens of pera; after my grandmother was laid to rest in her spot in eyüp cemetery my mother gave her clothes to the poor but made sure to snip the swallow buttons off her skirt suit first, one of them is still pinned to the collar of my jean jacket.

bogos usta is a womanizer my little darlings and don't you ever forget:

even when men get old

they keep on ogling girls

not just bogos but all men

they're always on the prowl for innocent young girls

because they're the easiest to trick

girls have to be careful about these kinds of things at all times

because the enemies of girls are many

they are slandered

eaten away by others' envy and spite

but the peacock protects you from the evil eye, heh?

and your mother protects you even from herself!

oh my little darlings

may good things await you

the places you visit with mother

are unforgettable my dears! heh?!;

why did your husband keep up his friendship with zeyyat even after you got married,,, and not once did he reproach you,,, or make a single snide comment,,, truth be told he was perfectly dignified about it,,, you still don't get it, the nature of that love,,, my sister said he was too proud to do anything,,, he surprised you,,, and he was never jealous either,,, when i said to him, sabit i have to tell you, i think i'm in love with zeyyat he laughed,,, well it can't be helped now can it no worries, still you won't deprive me of your friendship will you, he said,,, of course not, i said, we wouldn't even think of it, you're our closest friend are you not,,, he thanked me,,, what a bastard, i said to myself, he didn't even bat an eye,,, i'll show you i said,,, but i never knew what he was really thinking,,, he's devious i know that much,,, devious,,, maybe even back then he was already fattening up his id, thinking, i'll drive you two apart in the end anyway, you'll see...

***

handsome bogos has gotten a reputation for being the local robert taylor!

yet the pogrom of september 6th and 7th 1955 lies in wait at the door of the mirrored arcade

bogos usta is going to leave turkey too, just like the others...

the others

koço dimitri, his shop at number 1

rafael lami at number 10

aris usta at number 11

who sold yellow dust rags, öküzbaş laundry blue, floor wax, razor blades, back scratchers, kaol metal polish

but he never left

i was born and raised here, this is my homeland too he said, and moved to a small shop in hazzopulo arcade...

we still greet each other

at number 12 sarkis usta and his son fransua

at number 13 moiz pizante, from him mother bought a fez-colored robe de chambre for uncle

at number 15 rupen usta

he and simento ruso ended up moving to a building in the fish market together, at number 16 hristo the pleater!

the very same hristo usta who brought

the first pleating machine to turkey

what meaningful trades people took up in those days, isn't that so

my dear readers

chock-full of colorful yarn

those ustas left me awestruck

i'll never forget them

i still shop at their stores

hristo usta placed that pleated skirt

marilyn wore in *the seven year itch*

in his shop window

i have no idea why

still

as she was passing over a street grate

and that pleated skirt

billowed up

blown by the wind from below

men's hearts leapt

thinking they might catch a glimpse of marilyn's you-know-what

but with one hand she coyly held down her skirt!

that blondie sought out her existence in mirrors

it was a time when femininity raked in the cash
the more feminine she became the more wealthy she got
the wealthier she got the more pitiful she became
in the mirrored arcade at night
she would strut in front of the full-length mirrors
mounted to the arcade's columns
back and forth
as if before her were not a mirror
but a man to be seduced she smiled
at her own appearance
a bit like my mother when she flirted with the shop clerks
the statues of women in the upper floor niches
goddess of cuntery freckled nahide
the scales of justice hanging from her hand
goddess of the afterlife phony züleyha
goddess of the heavens shrill ruhiye
lüks nermin spinning the thread of life
goddess of music terfiye the shrew
goddess of mischief melahat of çanakkale
shimmying banu of the tray hugging sheaves of wheat
goddess of love sudsy mefkûre
goddess of peace whip-wielding saliha

leucothea the girl from the marsh croft

hair soaking wet just emerged from the sea

the twenty-two goddesses lined up in the niches

would marvel at marilyn

circe the sorceress

would call out to her

marilyn, marilyynnn!

but marilyn never heard

never managed to find the time to understand

anyone but herself

or this world of ours before whose mirrors

she floundered for years

until the kennedy brothers

destroyed

the visible part of her

the truth is you always wanted to free yourself from sabit,,, but you couldn't do it,,, he wouldn't let you,,, i'll have them both on a string he was thinking perhaps his private sorrow having transformed into resolve,,, worthless pieces of my world that's what i'll make you,,, or perhaps wickedness never so much as crossed his mind,,, we'll live together all hunky-dory like brothers and sisters he thought,,, yes, that's right, his inner voice always remained a mystery to you,,, perhaps it was this unknowability that attracted you,,, okay but now you can't possibly know zeyyat either,,, he too has shut his crown gate to you,,, what thoughts run through his mind,,, and what about yours,,, or could it be that you're the one playing the two of them,,, saying i'll have them both on a string alright,,, oh, no, that's not like you at all,,, it's true you desired the other one more,,, you started sleeping with him right after he got out of prison,,, sabit would just wait for you two never saying a word,,, what kind of a man behaves like that,,, he's madly in love with me,,, that's what you told yourself,,, but he was keeping you beneath his slotted sunshades, his slivered canopies,,, no,,, yes,,, sabit knew exactly what he was doing when he got between you two,,, he split you up,,, but hadn't you made the decision that day yourself,,, you told zeyyat, i think i have to go back to sabit he took your hand into his,,, he was dumbfounded,,, oh human mind,,, what happened to you,,, what happened to you to make you go back to sabit all of a sudden,,, please i'm begging you try to understand you said,,, zeyyat stood up,,, don't worry,,, it's not like i'm going to go kill myself or anything, i'll survive this too,,, and just like that you and zeyyat became the best of platonic friends,,, you knew perfectly well even as you told him about your decision that you didn't love sabit,,, damn the human brain that tiny walnut,,, thousands of years it's been since the founder of our world's first religion the prophet abraham set foot on this earth,,, i mean the creator of the concept of crime as we know it,,, and you, woman, why the devil do you insist on finding the truth,,, which truth,,, but you should know,,, yes that's right, one should know as much as one can,,, and go as far as she can go...

***

when a child sees herself in the mirror for the first time, does she know

that it's her self she sees?

does she say, whoa! that's me!

i don't think she can

the mirrors in that house in fener are always hung up high

in the bathroom above the sink

an old mirror

its surface mottled with clusters of mosquito-colored stains

no one ever bothered to pick her up and show her that mirror

it still baffles me why they hang mirrors up so high

too high for children to see themselves in.

until she encounters herself in one, she has no idea that such a thing as a "mirror" exists in the world

and yet it's perhaps only when she sees herself in it

that the child gradually comes to understand

that she's different from the adults around her, that she's a child

and even then she doesn't understand it not entirely

when i first looked into a mirror

it was my mother i saw not myself, my dear brothers and sisters, and don't ask me what that's supposed to mean,,,

i was in her bedroom,,,

she was sitting on the stool in front of her dressing table

admiring herself with a smile on her face

baring her teeth like tralala in the mirror

then zipping her lips back up

turned her face this way and that, gazing at her mirror-self

there were two mothers in the room

when i tried to climb into the lap of the one in the mirror i couldn't hold on and slid down a child

wanting yet unable to climb into her mother's lap

then i turned to this other mother the one in the flesh

who reached out and pulled me onto her lap and said,

"see that baby right there, that's you

lahzen, heh!"

i must've been how old at the time, i don't know, mother used to say i started walking early, at ten months!

at age two i began singing songs i'd heard on the radio

i listened as she told me countless tales about myself,,, who knows maybe she was making it all up,,,

that baby trying to climb onto the lap of the mother in the mirror

reaching out to the mirror with her tiny hands

reaching out again and again

scratching at the mirror's surface

slipping

falling

reaching out to the mirror again

slipping again

constantly reaching out to the mother in the mirror

an image hammered into the memory

two mothers, two children in the mirror

i've no idea why i'm telling you all this my dear readers

i can't know

i feel like i should know everything

before putting my other foot in the grave

what is it i should know, my truth of course, that's what

sure, my truth may be of no interest to you

but hell, i'm human too aren't i

which is why

whenever i think of the mirrored arcade

it's my mother's dressing table that comes to mind

and a baby constantly reaching out

to her mother in the mirror

never quite able to catch hold of her

but let me bring the mirrored arcade chapter to a close:

it changed hands after 1955

when we chased away the infidels

the watchman was a man called blind şerif

we uprooted the greeks

from these lands they'd called home for millennia

we drove them out

took their place but you see

this was the first, the most elegant european-style arcade

we turks had ever laid eyes on

stretching from the fish market to constitutionalism avenue

settled inside their niches

once we'd chased them—the greeks—away

they closed the arcade for a while

soon thereafter we turks occupied their shops

all the mythological figures were removed from their places

to be cleaned, they said

from their colorful hands we wrested

all the greek goddesses of the crafts the entire cast

demeter

dike

artemis

aphrodite

circe

we snatched away

those goddesses who play the lyre

spin silk thread

ruffles and tassel fringe

table runners

in the end the artisans of buttons and tassels

were left without yarn, belts, pompoms

without runners or ruffles

when reopened years later

the mirrored arcade

all that remained

was marilyn's pleated white skirt

in hristo usta's shop window

its white now blotched with purplish rot

the keys to the shop window

remained with hristo usta

hristo usta who fled to athens

do you think he'll come back

one day

you never know

they miss it here

once, when i was browsing the shop window of a jeweler in rhodes a man came out, walked up to me and said, you're turkish aren't you, yes? i said. me too but we were kicked out of our country. we lived in tarabya, turks, greeks, they were the best years of my childhood, how i yearn for those days now; even today i could describe the entire seafront to you, down to the very last rock.

can't you go back?,,, i asked,,, his eyes welled up with tears,,, i can't, you people broke my heart,,, i swore i'd never set foot there again as long as i live. then he pulled me into his shop, i'll fix you a cup of coffee, he said. i drank it. i apologized for everything we put them through,,, i told him about vangel, my childhood love. i gave him my address and said let's meet up should you forgive us and come back one day. he hugged me, kissed my cheeks and said, you look just like my childhood love münevver. we parted, both of us in tears. suddenly i turned around and asked, how did you know i was turkish, how could i not! he said, i see hundreds of faces looking into my shop window every day none of them peer inside quite like turks do. that made absolutely no sense to me but i said goodbye and walked off. i never went down that street again.

bedros' buttons at number 17

florist jirair at number 20 died

two young turkish women landed his shop

mayk's buttons at number 19, vahe did good business there, he was with number 22's mother mrs. hermann, these days it looks like one of those shops that sells fake perfume.

at number 21 on the right when you enter from the fish market

the chechen miliski brothers

who make fantastical bouquets but also funeral wreaths for "the church of three altars"

number 22 was once the garbis brothers' mezze shop

then it became a snack stall mother said

and onward she marched her red cuban-heeled shoes beating against the white marble floor of the european arcade

this floor here isn't made of any old marble

it's actually italian pisante

a different sort of marble

"so is there a cistern under here too mom?"

"why no, my pet, you think you'll find water under every marble floor?" as she passed by sarkis usta's shop she looked in the display window mirror and fluffed up her red hair with her gloved hands "heh!." "our courtyard's something special" she said. "whoever thought of it, well, good on them, it keeps us cool all summer, and if a war does break out we won't be going thirsty,,, we'll just open up the iron lid and drop a bucket inside..." "is there going to be a war?" my sister asked, "no darling, i'm just saying! heh? but then again, you never know; kings in olden times put a lot of thought into what might happen to them if,,, you know; kopsi kefali! heh? kopsi kefali!... those kings protected the people so they'd protect them back!.."

"are we the people?" i asked,

"of course we are, what else would we be!"

"is it a bad thing, to be the people?"

"why would it be bad, sweetheart, what kind of question is that?"

"but is there anything better than being the people?"

"oh for goodness sake! there you go again poking around under every rock and stone!" she said tugging me along by the hand. "better than the people,,, the thought of it!..."

we walked out of the same door we'd come in through, the one facing the british consulate.

swinging her hips

she walked toward the main street,

mother in front me in the middle my sister bringing up the rear we snaked our way through the narrow confines of aznavur arcade brushing past the rows of shops, emerging just across from the british consulate, from there we walked to tepebaşı, toward the old istanbul dram theater, yet something else we turks reduced to ashes...

the offices of *tan*

hüseyin cahit yalçın's newspaper,

şan cinema

atatürk cultural center

madımak hotel

and the statue of pir sultan in front of it

prisons together with the prisoners inside

the dram theater why did they burn them all to the ground

the republic's earliest generations

first encountered

children's plays

at the tepebaşı dram theater

and only later dramas

and comedies,

the dram theater in fact

was burnt down

because it was built on top of a muslim cemetery

our school took us there once

to a play in which ferih egemen's

"please take me along too

make me laugh till i cry

if i act out and upset you

you can beat me till i die..."

got pounded into our heads, that little red palace

with its curtains, fold upon fold of velvet

gilded mirrors

haunted balconies

scarlet-carpeted stairs

maroon velvet seats

it was as if they'd turned my mother into a theater

her star-studded eyes

childhood has never known

the eruptive joy of encountering a live spectacle

herds of "pyromaniacs"

destroying

piece by piece

what remains of our past

they'll turn us all into cobbler talip

a person without a past

in germany

he lived and died a stranger to that country

we, in our own country

those societies have their statues

constant reminders of the past

works of art

sculptures bursting out everywhere you look, above ground, below ground.

but what of our grandchildren

"them" "the others"!

who

are our others

the others' we

who is it trying to turn us into cobbler talip

each and every one of us

cobbler ahmet talip

was related to uncle apparently

and germany and turkey were brethren supposedly

since enver pasha's time

the germans took hundreds of "orphaned turkish apprentice children" from our orphanages

these were the days of war

of famine

gnawing broomsticks, grazing

licking tree trunks

when turks were defeating the enemy

the germans fed the small sunken stomachs

of "turkishorphanapprenticechildren" regardless of whether they were turkish kurdish alevi armenian

with cabbage, collards, potatoes, and beetroot grown in snow,,,

germany

gave each a golden ticket

and so you see that most famous the very first of the "turkishorphanapprenticechildren" cobbler ahmet talip, clutching cabbages to his chest, full of gratitude to that country

got his start by patching the soles of the down-and-out

from those of little sabahattin the newspaper boy

to the soles of hrant

all his life

quietly

finishing his apprenticeship becoming a master

bearing within himself like a secret religion

the proletariat dictatorship of the future

a cobbler until 1983

he even went before the god of shoes

bearing the finest hand-crafted footwear

he spent his life

tirelessly patching his gravestone

patch upon patch

when news of his passing arrived from germany

uncle took to the streets again

a bottle of marmara wine in his hand

his breath echoing back from the heavens

"the gospodars! the gospodars!"

as if he wanted to be reunited with his great unknown

it was then that we witnessed for the first time how he was capable of sadness like a human being and now yes he was leaving

with that alexander kaidanovsky stare

like in tarkovsky's *stalker*

looking for the "room of happiness"

he'd frequent

the meyhane

next to yervant the piano repairman's shop in fener

that "room of happiness"

was in fact the room of happiness

tarkovsky was in search of

symbolizing the dictatorship of the proletariat

spellbound as we watched the film

zeyyat and i hand in hand

how

nice it was to feel his firm grip

the whole film long

he was sitting on my right

at the emek cinema

every now and then i'd glance at his handsome profile

and he'd turn and smile at me

the lines of his hands so like the lines of my own

my mother rushing out into the streets in the middle of the night to look for uncle

finding

that desperate rage

like a man returning from years of breaking rocks in the aşkale labor camp

forlorn his arm linked in my mother's

she led him away out of our sight

that jackass who just wouldn't die

doting on him as they stumbled along

saying, uncle! oh uncle! uncle my dearest don't despair, there's nothing to be done

and that man

uncle

she pitied and loved as if

he were all alone, the sole survivor of wars of exploitation

compassionately

erasing my father

perhaps

uncle too was one of those

men without a past

but we did not forget our father

and one day slipped poisonous mushrooms into uncle's soup

snow-white nubs that had sprung up in the garden

watch out they're poisonous they'd told us

we picked and mashed them up

mother was out

he ate it

we waited

no one's ever survived after eating these mushrooms, my sister said

uncle lay down on the couch in the courtyard

drifted into eternal sleep

we're free, we rejoiced

but he stirred back to life toward evening

his death

would come later

as he walked down the hill in sancaktar bottle in hand

and slipped on the icy street

fell and cracked his head open

the shards of glass thorns sticking out of the scourge's face

as for ahmet talip

back then we couldn't have known

the difference between the death of a worker without a past

and that of a worker with one

in our home, the blackout curtains uncle had hung from spring-loaded pulleys drawn closed

in those days when we struggled to fathom

a life

we were unable to make sense of yet

what if i had zeyyat's child but told sabit it was his,,, would he catch on? of course not,,, the baby would be the child of a sinful woman,,, but why would i do that,,, the thoughts that pass through a person's mind,,, out of the blue,,, out of the blue you say,,, it's incredible, the coercive power of that thing called civilization,,,

***

seems that the house in küçüksu where aunt lived was where father once lived too,,, on its walls hung childhood family photos, mother and father so very very young,,, father, a wiry man, closer in appearance to my sister than me; thick black hair, mossy eyes,,, farthest in the back, even bigger than uncle; a hulking giant of a man, his wings spread over the entire family,,, my sister said, see that's bigbeargramps when he was young,,, i hadn't been born yet so i'm not in the picture,,, my sister's such a beautiful little girl, light brown curls glinting on her shoulders, huge hazel eyes; smiling, leaning her head against mother's skirt,,, she's got the voice of a soprano, but mine is a coloratura, uncle said that coloratura sopranos are prized all the more,,, i said to my sister, why don't we have any pictures of dad at our place,,, because mom's in love with that monster now or haven't you noticed? she said.

***

the sea,,, the golden horn,,, in every direction the sea, a horizontal blue wall blocking passage to the other side,,, along the shore city ferries like adorable toys approach and pull away from the quay,,, who are the owners of this place,,, the very first owners,,, could it be the descendants of italians, the greeks of roman heritage, the latins or the ancient greeks,,, maybe the noblemen of fener,,, or the enlightened mavrogenis family, perhaps the kantakouzenoses, or bezirgân the banker,,, the mavrocordatoses,,, they're all underground now

to get here go down from eğrikapı to yedikule, turn at the slaughterhouse, narlıkapı yenikapı kadırga... make your way from topkapı çemberlitaş to fatih, yavuzsultanselim then kocamustafapaşa,,, with their walls and boundaries, other sides, passageways, people of so many lineages here,,, no one here's a local,,, no one anywhere's a local,,, the true locals are the folks buried underground, the ones aboveground are all foreigners,,, the true locals are the ones buried yet another layer farther down below the true locals,,, and the even more local locals are buried down below them,,, half of us are down below beneath the city, the other half of us are here but soon enough we'll be down below and the newcomers will be up above,,, the newcomers will putter about aboveground like we did before they join us,,, they'll wait their turn,,, obsessing over what's below,,, like us they'll wonder about hades, about the ferryman,,, driving death and obliteration from their thoughts they'll try to lead free and easy lives but won't ever succeed, that deep "anxiety" will never relinquish its grip,,, the one they say søren first struck upon,,, they'll be hounded by the question "how will i cease to exist",,, there's nothing in the afterworld my mother says, this world is all we've got,,, so let's make the most of it and not be in a rush,,, ashes to ashes, dust to dust, no more no less,,, clacking her heels against the marble floor she starts dancing the farandole,,, it's through dance that mother escapes death,,, as for me no matter where i am i get the urge to go somewhere else,,, the other side someplace i know nothing about,,, that's where i need to go,,, the other side, always beyond,,, why have i never felt at home in these lands,,, unbeknownst to me that demon called uncle burrowed into my pores,,, like how unbeknownst to himself abraham wanted to kill his son,,, but i was fully in the know of my desire to destroy uncle,,, oh and how!,,, couldn't do it though...

søren's book has several different versions of the sacrifice scene. one of them is a confession and we can read it as the universal essence of the book or of what it means to be human.

taking isaac with him, he starts making his way to mount moriah. isaac clings to abraham's knees, he beseeches him at his feet, abraham raises isaac up,,, abraham walks beside isaac, his words full of consolation,,, but isaac understands him not,,, for a moment he pulls away from abraham and when he looks at him again,,, verily

"abraham's face had changed. a wild look flashed in his eyes. his bodily form was dreadful. he grabbed isaac by the throat and threw him to the ground. he said to him, 'you stupid boy, do you think i'm your father? i'm an idolator. do you think this is god's command? no, this is what i desire...'" (søren kierkegaard, "fear and trembling"—dialectical lyric. turkish translation n. ekrem düzen. ara publishing. first edition 1990)

***

when aunt died we ran into people we knew from our childhood, in the courtyard of the backstreet mosque with 1836 inscribed over its door. all of them were stooped over; all of them seemed to be looking for something they'd dropped,,, apparently only able to recognize each other from their shoes, they peered at one another's feet as they scooted from person to person falling into conversation all wearing old thick-soled shoes, it was they who were the first generation to suffer the full brunt of postwar life. once in a while the sprier of the bunch would crane their necks as far as their necks could crane which afforded from an acute angle a partial view of the person opposite them. but none of them were able to recognize us from our shoes; we were young women who wore moccasins now,,, not belkıs abla of yenimahalle legendary for her beauty or sahure hanım, nor mother kıymet, aunt hafize, avram the tinsmith, barber necati or filly fatma,,, why were they like that,,, duh, the bosphorus winds! you think it's easy to live in a giant wooden house with a wood-burning stove, my sister said. you've never lit a stove in your life, how would you know!

***

at aunt's place they ate fish almost every day. do you, my sister said, remember andon effendi. his back was bent, curved, bowed! just like the bow-shaped strip of wood he used to carry his baskets of fish. you mean aunt's you-know-who? andon effendi was the local fish peddler, aunt would buy her fish from him. one time uncle hasan the coachman said to mother in hushed tones, "when he was in greece he was one of the guerrillas who went up into the mountains." but we heard him. my sister asked our aunt, "what does guerrilla mean, auntie," i don't know i've never heard the word before, where'd you hear it? "i came across it in a book!" i'll ask uncle, my sister said.

cooing "freeesh fiiish" andon effendi would pull aside the wet newspapers he placed over his baskets and take a peek at aunt's legs. "they look lovely!" she'd say every single time, picking and choosing from among the colorful fish flopping on top of one another, snatching them up one by one, holding tightly onto the fish squirming in the palm of her hand she'd raise it up close to her face and say, "think you can get away from me now do you?" and then toss the fish onto the tray sultan held out as she stood there waiting beside her. aunt and andon effendi would laugh together,,, andon effendi was the only person she laughed with,,,

aunt in her final days, apurum, puriam, porom,,, pacing around her room murmuring, no more fish, andon's gone, fish are all gone, then settling into her old throne she'd ramble on, sultan girl where the hell are you, don't make me come after you, i haven't kicked the bucket yet you know.

you're writing, you keep going on and on about that circus of a childhood you cannot forget, it's from there you wish to extract the essence of truth; but what is it you really want to say? why are you so hung up on stones,,, you can't figure out how göbeklitepe came to be put into place by human hands back in the 9000s bc,,, how could those stones,,, an experiment of seven thousand years of hegemonic social classes, the sumerians and their city-states, uruk the world's first metropolis,,, tablets, cuneiform, revered temple prostitutes wearing headscarves, mary impregnated by a glance, the world's male and female prostitutes impregnated by sunlight, impregnated by moonlight, impregnated by forbidden fruit, the tower of babylon rising up for a chat with god, destroyers nebuchadnezzar... is it possible to start all over again? and if it were, how do you know the outcome wouldn't always be exactly the same! why on earth are you so passionate about stones,,,

they're driving you insane,,, you should know that,,, what is it with you and your passion for creations from the time of slavery,,, what a contradiction,,, as if slavery no longer exists in our world,,, why this passion for the eternal magnificence of ancient civilizations? for that which is permanent,,, why this soft spot for magnificence,,, for creations from the time of slavery,,, for the ceramic tiles of hüsrevpaşa mosque,,, for the colosseum through which rivers of blood once flowed,,, for the coemeterium,,, you couldn't care less about the carthaginian prisoners who worked themselves half to death in the quarries mining the stones used to build the temple of zeus,,, when humanity starts all over again it's going to end up at the exact same spot,,, the colosseum,,, it will create the torah and class society along with it and arrive all over again at the coemeterium, the pyramids, the ziggurat, rublev's bell,,, oratorios,,, requiems,,, another isaac another prophet abraham,,, again with the messiah,,, and you're still hoping to capture the hidden essence of truth in your childhood,,, you think that finding it will fix the future,,, truth has no essence, no substance, no ember, no eye,,, enough with the stones,,, the inscription that the stone wrote upon itself on the column of theodosius also said to have been erected by cleopatra, you cannot forget that inscription for the life of you, why?

***

formerly it (was) difficult to obey noble masters (but)

(i) was ordered

to bear the wreath of victory over dead tyrants.

all bow down to theodosius and his eternal

offspring

thus in thirty-two days (i) was prevailed over

and in the time of praefectus proklos

was (i) raised toward the skies

***

uncle hasan's carriage would be waiting for us at the quay when the ferry arrived in küçüksu. the name of the ferry may have been suhulet, paşabahçe, fenerbahçe, or dilnişin. before drawing up to the quay, the ferry would trace an arc, veering so close to küçüksu palace we could almost reach out and touch its seaside gardens, the steps leading down to the sea where the sultan's rowboats docked, the sash bars of the windows facing the sea, the reliefs in between, the rooftop friezes.

we were much fonder of our aunt then, back when she used to take us in during the holidays.

from time to time she'd have uncle hasan hitch up the buggy. we'd climb in and go for a ride around küçüksu, take the lower road to the backstreet neighborhood and go to the fairgrounds in the meadow at the end of göksu creek, in what was known as the greek neighborhood. during this festive time of christian holy days in september the sacred spring would be swarming with people. aunt too believed the spring's water to be blessed, so she'd take us to the small church and have us drink from it. back then the water spurted from the ground even, and it was back then we saw for the very first time fairground shows, tightrope walkers, and a midget rolling around on the ground like a ball.

bathed in sweat, mother was splitting open the bellies of eggplants, "you two go upstairs and play, sultan and i are going to put this on the stove, but don't disturb your aunt, she's doing her prayers in her room."

as soon as we set foot in the room our eye was caught by a white silk handkerchief shored up with lace lying on the corner table. one of its folds was askew, revealing the edge of a piece of paper. picking up the handkerchief my sister paused for a moment then quickly unfolded it revealing a letter which she read to me in a single breath:

"my dear lady, oh how i pine for göksu creek, how i adore every inch of the place, would give my life for it, its gravestones even. when i think of that chestnut tree we sat under, i can't help but weep. my dear, i would give anything to be back there. god will strike down those who called us infidels and tore us apart and before i die i will return and come back to you. why did they drive us away, our brothers in god here don't like us either. they call us 'the spawn of turks,' nothing's going good here, my dear lady, only that we don't fear for our lives. i kiss those hands with which my good lady firmly caught hold of my fresh live fish. hadji andon."

shaken, my sister folded the letter back up into the handkerchief and put it back on the table. we stared at one another our eyes wide with shock. don't you dare tell anyone about this! she said, we're going to take this secret to the grave, got it? i won't say a word, i said, were they, you know, a thing? i said, of course, don't you get it? my sister said, nobody else can find out about this, if they do we'll be done for! of course i won't tell, even thinking of them now makes me want to cry i said, somewhat scared; oh why! at every turn these constant companions of mine fear, sadness, and trembling!.. as if i myself were the innocent son abraham was about to "set ablaze for god"...

later we sat in front of the window in threadbare pearl-grey armchairs and sulked staring at the sea, at the colors coursing into the white clouds dipping into the blue of its waters. looking out over izzet's gardens it was as if i could sense the majestic landward palace gate, newly painted a gleaming white, and a new heart that had settled into place, plastered over with the tenderest of emotion; our poor aunt and hadji andon...

an ashen light of times of old was falling over the panorama which encompassed part of küçüksu creek, rumeli fortress, and the faint silhouette of the cemetery, i snuggled up to my sister and said, sis i love auntie all the more now. me too, she said and hugged me.

uncle never came to küçüksu. neither aunt nor bigbeargramps wanted him to.

since we knew uncle hasan loved children and that he was a good man, without us even realizing it feelings akin to goodness stirred within us and we started to see ourselves as good kids,,, among the carriages with spring suspension that ran along the bosphorus, uncle hasan's was one of the most beautiful. even the carriages on the islands paled in comparison. shaded by a tasseled canopy in the summer and enclosed with an embroidered tarpaulin in the winter, this resplendent carriage, even fancier than the buggy, with its wooden paneling adorned with colorful reliefs of flowers and always smelling of fresh varnish, is a lovely snapshot of my life, perhaps a vignette of my truth.

you made him a cup of nescafé and took it to him,,, his back is turned to you, his hair's grown white; he has a shapely skull that suits his shoulders, his ears are translucent under the morning light, pink ears long and thick; when viewed from the front hair sprouts from within, grass sprouting from between pebble mosaics,,, grass white and thick, in astounding abundance,,, they left a tiny hole to let the air in; he says he has the barber singe them occasionally, and the ones sprouting out of his nose he trims himself; the ears hear just fine, he's ten years older than me...

***

may 6th, the day of the feast of saint george

whom uncle hung on the wall of the house in fener

may 6th, the day when the junta of march 12th ended the lives of deniz gezmiş, hüseyin inan, and yusuf aslan by execution.

may 6th, the day of hızırilyas

or hıdırellez, that is

in the manuscript "wonders of creation," hazrat ali

on horseback wielding a spear

the spitting image of saint george

slaying the dragon

in the tenth century akdamar church

and these depictions existed in other churches too;

in the twelfth century danishmendid coins

also showed a mounted horseman wielding a spear

– do you know? my sister said, how we escaped being burnt to death that day

– in the mosque you mean?

– yes, i was the one who rescued all of you from being burnt to death in the mosque that day

– how?

– it just happened

– how?

– through prayer,,, remember the one aunt made us memorize "the prayer that burns the devil and puts out his fire": "eûzü bi'kelimâtillahittammâti..."

– yes yes min şerri mâ haleka...

– ve zerae

– wahahaha! how funny is that, "ve berae ve min şerri..." i've forgotten the rest

– well i haven't and i recited it and all of a sudden the devil's fire went out before it even got started and he keeled right over

– but we didn't see any devil lying there!

– you wouldn't, only the person praying would...

– sis i'm not a child anymore you know!

– fine don't believe me, but tell me this, why didn't they torch us then

– you know how they said the army was on its way, soon as word got out they got scared and ran off

– what army nobody came

– well it turned out to be a lie the army wasn't on its way, someone made it up, the others got scared and ran away...

– right, 'cause they were scared!

– forget it sis you believe what you want and i'll believe what i want

– look do i go around meddling in your life no, so don't you go trying to change me,,, you spent all those years studying got yourself a university degree and for what to lock yourself away at home with that lout,,, what in the world got into you sis,,, and now you're in complete denial of our entire past,,, as if you weren't the one who was in love with efthim how could you change so much even thinking of you makes me want to cry. it's a good thing you're so far away and we can't see each other much. besides you say you're happy with your husband so i don't really worry...

***

the watchman of the mirrored arcade was a man they called blind şerif. a man who could perceive and see everything through sound. when in 1955 menderes and celâl bayar with their battle cry proclaimed that the infidel greeks had planted a bomb in atatürk's home, all the lumpen were unleashed onto pera: they broke the windows facing the british consulate and clambered into the arcade. they clubbed the watchman blind şerif on the head knocking him out; blind şerif used to sleep at number 10, on the second floor of the mirrored arcade in the room between the goddess of bounty and the goddess of knowledge the same floor where the painter komet's studio is right now (2005) painter komet who paints canvases with poetry and poetry with canvases

blind şerif came to, he recognized the looters not by sight but by sound, for some reason they didn't kill him, he's still alive but they ransacked the mirrored arcade. they took to the streets,,, silks, wools, french linen, gabardine serge and caddice, all dragged down independence street,,, underpants, muddied pajamas, glassware, baccarat crystal, you can't bear to look,,, handmade,,, lung-made bloodied mouth-blown bottles and shoes and a man clad in potur pants wrapped in a shimmering umber beaverskin coat is making an escape green plastic buckets wedged under his arm,,, lebon's cakes,,, and those of unequal religion thrashed and beaten on independence street,,, priests circumcised with bread knives,,, all to the point they sold off house and home to our people for next to nothing, the hell we put them through to drive them into the four corners of the earth...

it was they who in the "evliya çelebi travelogue," during the tenth siege before mehmed the conqueror captured istanbul:

"(...) 'during the tenth siege' (...) upon khan bayezid the thunderbolt's ascendance to the throne as the sole sultan,,, when the tekfur king accepted his proposal of peace the thunderbolt garrisoned twenty thousand men in istambol from edirne gate, the crooked gate and the gate of eba eyyub el-ensari, filling istambol with mohammedans all the way from unkapanı to zeyrek-başı, karaman and again back to edirne gate,,, through cibali gate,,, what they call rose mosque, and the nearby sirkejhi dervish lodge he made into a court of justice. he garrisoned galata tower alone with six thousand men, such that the mohammedans overtook half of galata, all the way up to the tower, occupying half of islambol over by the haghia sophia and there was no strife between any of the infidels and the mohammedans..."

***

gone would be the ashen emotions of winter, its blacks and whites wiped away, the scent of the earth slowly rising up, wormwood, centaurium, dandelions, daisies, a thousand and one different wildflowers, globe thistles drifting in the air, as daylight peers into all the furled bodies; the school holiday would begin, the dance floor would be readied, the neighborhood kids flocking into our white marble courtyard like storklings. at which point mother would go down to the kitchen to make the dough for her famed mahaleb cookies and sweet rolls then hand us the trays and send us over to refet's bakery: "the oven's sure to be red-hot right now, so just wait there till they're ready and come straight back" she'd tell us. instead we'd leave the trays at the bakery and go to the patriarchate to light candles my sister would tuck some money into my hand, "go ahead and light one c'mon i know all about vangel" she'd tell me. vangel was so sweet, such a darling; warm-hearted, never sparing of himself, the kind of person others sought out to lean their souls upon and weep for a while,,, vangel grab that trash on your way out and toss it into the sea why don't you they'd tell him, and he'd dash to the shore and dash right back again,,, last winter when we were snowed in and the streets were covered in ice, he picked me up and whisked me off all the way down from our front door to the bottom of the hill on the sled he'd made out of one of his father's orange crates,,, i scrunched in behind him but didn't hold on, "hang on to me or you'll fall off!" he said, i wrapped my arms around his waist, burying my face in his back, and he whisked me away,,, my cheek got all scratched up by the raw wool sweater aunt vara had knit for him. "what in the world happened to you?" mother asked "what sort of wool could rub my little girl's face raw like that!" and pulled me onto her lap.

***

we're gonna nail that boar this time he's not getting away, uncle said, the picture of saint george he'd hung on the wall of the courtyard awaking in the mind,,, lacking only horse and machete, his voice roaring, his left eye squinted real tight

– the shells are ready, the buckshot, dumdum bullets everything's ready it's going to be a fine hunt this time around.

– how about you drop this boar hunting business, mother said.

– never! he said, stroking his gun, already got the "buttshot" loaded! it's gonna be a driven hunt, we're gonna get him good this time. i'll bring you all back a piece

– no thanks, mother said, i don't want a piece of some giant hairy animal in my house, don't you dare i won't let you bring it in here i'm telling you!

uncle returned empty-handed! with him was a thirteen-year-old boy with rabble-rouser eyes and tattered cheeks.

– what the hell is this? said mother

– we hunted it down instead of the boar, name's isaac! uncle said bursting into one of his maddening laughs.

all together they'd climbed the mountain, mount mor near çiğli, while the villagers banged on tins to drive the boars toward them from the opposite direction. we'd never seen uncle in such a state; he kept blinking his eyes, as if trying to wake himself up, swiveling his head to look at me then mother then sister over and over again as he told us what happened. on our way to the summit we saw a dark figure ahead, he said looking at the boy,,, turned out to be some scruffy guy who was holding his hands up toward the sky praying and this boy, who was tied to a log on the ground watching him with a grin on his face,,, *the child asked, "father, where is the lamb for the burnt offering?",,, the man said, "don't worry my child, god himself will provide the lamb for the offering!"*

next to the man was a gigantic saw. we ran over to him and asked him what he was doing, he motioned for us to be quiet then whispered.

– what choice do i have at the command of my allah i'm about to give my child as a burnt offering to his path but isaac doesn't know what i'm about to do telling him would be tantamount to entrapping my allah, keep your voice down!

– are you crazy or what, get up come to your senses,,, quick untie the kid, what kind of a person strangles their own son?

– i'm not crazy my brother, it's not for me to disobey god's command

– let me show you a thing or two about that god of yours emrullah said, grabbing the guy by the collar.

the man jabbered on

– my god is testing me my brothers he's testing my faith in him there's nothing else i can tell you because you don't speak my language. i've submitted myself to my lord on high he appears to me every night he tells me to prove my faith to him, please brothers leave me be i'm begging you, pretend you never saw me, this is between me and my lord above, you guys go hunt your boar

– oh come on, god appears to him every night humph,,, you watch hamlet did you now picklepuss, petrus said

– hamlet you say! what, did my lord appear to him too?!

– doddering fool's made himself out to be a prophet, nurettin said

– why are we even talking to this lunatic let's untie the kid and turn this guy into the police, i said

– please my brothers, don't, god would never let me be, i have faith in him, besides my name is abraham! is there not some divine wisdom at play in all this, i mean my son's name is isaac! there's a lesson to be learned in all this; leave me be, you don't understand us, we're starved and destitute! my wife sarah's a day laborer, i gather food from the garbage, god could no longer bear to see me like this; he was ashamed that people had done this to me and this is how he penalized them for it!

– the words shut your trap we know your ilk all too well were barely out of my mouth when a dead boar suddenly came rolling down the slope and landed in front of us right at our feet. all of us nurettin, petrus, asım, bekir, and emrullah we all stood there staring. it had to have been one of the boars the americans at çiğli airbase shot during the driven hunt. they were out hunting the same day. abraham stood over the corpse of the boar trembling his eyes nearly popping out of his head. see you see it too so i was right, is this not a miracle of allah!..

– then why did he send you a boar instead of a lamb, aren't you muslim? said petrus.

– i am muslim brother, elhamdulilah. i pray five times a day

– alright fine take the boar and give us the kid.

the man looked at the boy then at us then at the boar.

– the kid's a good-for-nothing anyway you can have him. i know what my lord's trying to tell me

tears streamed down his face

– but how am i supposed to carry this giant boar home? he said

– same way you carried the log; by the same grace of that god of yours you can carry the boar too, said petrus.

all this time from underneath the firewood this isaac here kept grinning just like he is now. didn't say a word. the poor mute...

the villagers found us on our way back, told us the hunt had ended up serving the americans, that they'd done in two boars giving chase down the mountain tossed them into the jimmies and drove off and that another wounded boar had gotten away.

– didn't you guys get anything? one of them asked

no, we all replied, we didn't

emrullah,

– how come these infidels eat boar when they could be having lamb?

– 'cause it's delicious and more nutritious, petrus said, maybe muslims would be smarter if they ate it too!!

– oh come on now don't get offended, it's out of habit! emrullah said, the way we say "infidel" all the time, sorry about that...

as we were leaving one of the villagers yelled after us,,, where'd you find that little bastard!.. then he turned around and disappeared from sight!

mother leapt to her feet. she went upstairs and withdrew to her room. my sister and i looked at isaac again. his thick hair flowing down onto his shoulders, his eyes of pale blue. he was a beautiful child.

– what the hell are you two gawking at, never seen a child before? he said to us

– oh look he can speak! but you said he was mute!..

– well that son of a bitch! how should i know, that f..ker that's supposed to be his father said he was. he tricked us that prick! uncle walked up to the boy, got real close. why the hell didn't you speak till now you goddamn clod. then at a loss for words he looked around blankly the child was wearing the same grin he'd had on when he arrived...

– go on now up to your rooms time for bed, uncle said.

he put isaac to sleep on the couch in the courtyard that night. in the morning isaac was gone he'd run away...

***

we're back home after fetching the trays from the bakery. mother's fixed up the table with daisies and carnations from the garden, "christos anesti—alithos anesti" we all chant as we tap our easter eggs together then out of the blue our aunt appears! and with that mother's dashed in saying "don't you dare go tapping your eggs in front of your aunt." she's turned up carrying an éclair-like dessert, what they call laz börek, rolls of flaky homemade filo pastry sweetened with milk and honey, and is ushered into the drawing room and given the royal treatment. auntie lefkothea meanwhile holding a large copper pot rimmed with flour, she places her "psito" a potato dish with a center of meat and pearl onions, in the center of the table, calls out to us "come on yavrimou sweetyhearts, dig in." we rush in. her face beaming with joy as she watches us, auntie roly-poly lefkothea alongside baldy waddles about in our midst.

spotting our aunt in the corner looking all high and mighty auntie lefkothea's face flushes red, she walks up and slaps her, says the nerve of you! showing up here, when not once did you invite me for a ride in that blasted buggy of yours, you useless hag, aunt collapses no one picks her up, she's shrinking slowly erased until she disappears completely...

mother keeps looking at the trace of aunt left on the floor starts laughing angrily then becomes a phantom pendulum laden with the emotions that are piled up inside her like mountain ranges, something we could never fathom,,, she's tapped the tip of her shoe against the lid of the dead history in the cistern patiently awaiting the day it will rise to haunt us and it freezes then and there...

***

mother's a musical instrument with broken strings when uncle isn't around, holding in her hand the book she keeps on her nightstand at all times its pages she's wilted by the spit on her finger every turn of the page,,, *letters from my windmill* is the title of the book; she isn't reading it though, she's filled her unstrummed heart with her silence,,, soundless words bubble up rising to her face,,, she'll be chewing on her nails, turned toward the window that opens out onto the garden, her eyes pulsing with the current of energy she longs to conceal; facing the rectangular window of the living room its curtains she's embroidered herself—*ören* bayan yarn and a size seventy crochet hook—what she sees is not the garden but rather childhood dreams overlaid with the ghosts of the farandole figures on the curtains she's knit a little girl's puffy silken dress her youthful mother tying a giant bow in her hair her father's bushy mustache scratching her face as he gives her a kiss, a happy family taking their darling little girl on a carriage ride,,, the circle dance the farandole with family relatives friends gathered together at their summer houses on special days,,, the original form of this dance was how sufi muslims, followers of jesus son of mary, would worship. forming two circles spinning round and round in opposite directions until one reaches a state of ecstasy,,, similar to what our dervishes do. but over time the circles broke apart and the dancers began doing their own thing in smaller groups or by themselves.

lahzen would feel her heart tremble as the entire floor of the wooden house shook beneath the stomping feet. she'd feel it all the father going off to war, the news of his death, the mother heart-broken and fearful falling asleep with her daughter wrapped in her arms, moving to istanbul, to fatih to be with their relatives,,, it seemed magical, this curtain; blowing gently in the wind the frolicking dancers would invite her to join the dance,,, squinting her eyes, she'd get up, place the tip of one of her red shoes, the ones she never took off, that she'd picked up from karakaş's store in mahmutpaşa, on the lid of the cistern there to the right just inside the courtyard as crisp and cool as a meadow,,, she'd listen to a rhythm drifting in from somewhere enraptured her body keeping time to the rhythm of that thing,,, her entire nervous system all its levers and pulleys its feminine and masculine motifs would begin to tremble all those tiny ripples merging, giving birth all of a sudden to a certain splendor—-tip-tippy-tap tap-tap-tap,,, and now here she is, eyes squeezed tightly shut, waiting for something,,, for whom you ask? for the dance troupe of kith and kin to come swarming in from avignon,,, the circle dancers from her childhood, those permanent fixtures of her mind.

she heard the sound of joyful voices; the whole of fener old and young alike had taken to the streets,,, here they come, musicians bearing shrill pipes, tambourines, drums, violins, cymbals, among them a young boy carrying a stringed instrument on his back,,, his kind eyes twinkling the boy charged ahead walking straight up to our door,,, he drew closer,,, it was efthim, and alongside him uncle petrus, bells and cymbals in hand, the two of them came inside,,, then all the children from our neighborhood followed by what seemed like all the peoples of the world, they swarmed inside too,,, from the four corners of our land the yörüks, turkmens, karapapakhs, yazidis, zazas, hemshin armenians, hemshin laz, chaldeans, kurds, the apurum, circassians, people in black hoods, burkas, men in blue turbans, young men wearing lenin caps, khaki jackets, and army boots, young men carrying a sculpture of jesus, others bearing statues of women saints, and then the saints themselves; saint lucia holding a lantern, she hasn't yet gouged her own eyes out, wrapped them up in a kerchief, and sent them to the man who accosted her because of her faith,,, she can still see, enveloping the entire earth with her big blue eyes, and she marches forth, a veritable ship's shroud of woman,,, saint felicitas, her seven sons have yet to be slaughtered before her very eyes, or she herself boiled alive in a cauldron on account of her faith,,, she's smiling,,, saint gonca kuriş smiles too, as she holds onto the noose of the hezbollah who hogtied her to death in cold blood,,, hrant dink walks among them his face beaming a dove perched on his arm,,, double-winged, four-winged, six-winged boy angels, girl angels, prissy-boy angels, hermaphrodites all rush inside,,,

on the brink of dancing my mother's eyes are narrowed but she's smiling at the guests,,, once again the tip of her shoe is on the lid of the cistern,,, eager to begin the dance she waits for all the neighbors to arrive,,, and they too slip in through her narrowed eyes,,, the phanariotes wearing masks to hide their identities,,, (though everyone can tell who they are) auntie havva, auntie lefkothea, auntie meryem, muhibbe hanım, ruhiye hanım, auntie vara, that old belarusian woman with her thick black braided hair whose name i can never pronounce, her head conified in a white turban, others flashing big smiles their teeth grains of rice, a young woman in a french baroque outfit makes her way through the crowd swinging her big butt, the country's number one mattress dancer; her outfit is a beige beaded skirt with a tail, and long lacy undies—during the farandole she'll lift up her skirt showing the children a wooden penis painted red which she's tied to her belly, then she'll grab it shaking it to the beat of the music, at which point everyone will be rolling on the floor laughing she alone will remain standing she'll wave the wooden penis at us in salute, before she leaves she'll take it off and toss it into the audience everyone will race to catch it as if it were a wedding bouquet and whoever does catch it will play that very same role wearing that very same outfit the following year,,, as more of them arrive our small marble courtyard expands, as more of them arrive, as more and more of them arrive the marble floor built by hadji murat, beneath which lies the cistern with the dead water where the egos live and breathe, expands until it's enveloping not only the grand halls of küçüksu palace and dolmabahçe but the entire hippod-rome, all together the german fountain, the serpent column, the walled obelisk, theodosius's monolith granite obelisk along with the bas-reliefs on its pedestal, they all, they all descend into the middle of the courtyard, settling onto the spina that cuts across it,,, is everybody in, asks uncle keeping one eye on mother as usual,,, once the courtyard had taken everyone but everyone but everyone in uncle ran over to mother who was oblivious as he lifted her leg off the cistern and gently placed it on the ground before unlocking the lid,,, and with that all the egos leapt out of the cistern scattering amongst us,,, they were invisible to the eye yet we neighborhood kids began screaming at the top of our lungs it's the egos the egos,,, they're all deaf to our screams, mother and everyone else,,, as if the ceiling isn't there at all mother stares into the pit of the dome that is the sky, seems to match the rippling of her body to that of the dome's spirit,,, uncle lowered a bucket into the cistern, the bucket hit the water with a "plunk," careful not to let the rope slip out of its groove he jerked the rope then let go jerked then let go and once he'd sensed that the bucket was full yanked it back up. the wine was red,,, he ladled it into cups and handed them around,,, gave us kids some too,,, we began to drink,,, he put the lid of the cistern back into place, closing it,,, mother hopped on and off the edge of the cistern right foot left foot right foot left foot, at that moment in place of herself she was a neighing tralala composed of dreams,,, just then the other musicians also rushed in hailing mother, "peace be upon our bride! peace,,, they too raised their mugs in a toast,,, mother swigged down the wine uncle had handed her and smashed the cup onto the ground,,, the coptic violinist who regularly made his rounds through the meyhanes of asmalımescit fiddled a few odd notes into mother's ear, madam anahit hit a key on her accordion,,, that's when, showering everyone with her grass-green eyes, mother centered herself in the middle of the hippodrome and started to dance,,, the musicians form a circle around her and around the musicians others join in forming a second circle, and one more and again together with her all of them together spinning in opposite directions around the spina they too began to dance,,, in her flared cornelian-cherry-red skirt, homeros-hued blouse, and red shoes, with her red lips, red nails, red hair, and red legs mother switched partners again and again spinning round and round till she became a spindle of fire while the rest of them all of them the masked women, girls, and boys alike enclosed her holding hands doing the farandole dancing and dancing till their feet lifted off the floor of the courtyard and they began floating up into the air,,, as they floated higher and higher the ceiling parted and the blue sky poured in,,, my sister held on to mother's skirt and i onto my sister screaming please don't go mum we spun in midair like that for some time,,, next thing we knew we were back on the ground,,, everyone had left,,, a little while later the musicians took off as well, playing their instruments flocking through the backstreets of fener all the way to the other side to pera,,, the music's coming from the other side from "burnt gate," mother said these musicians they're from "burnt castle," it's on the way to budapest, they're from way over there,,, hours later even we could still hear the sound of their music.

***

thus did the years pass there in the dominion of gog magog trudging forth alongside uncle, the neighbors, and ego, meanwhile the local boys and girls they had scattered to the seven climates four continents seventy-two peoples of the globe

as for me, they said i'd turned out to become a rather virtuous young woman, kind-hearted, gracious, who'd finished school gotten a job started earning money albeit not much and that the time had come for me to be delivered into a male embrace when

in a shotgun wedding i threw myself into the arms of a young man

my sister had arrived at that milestone several years earlier

with the son of a farming family from düzce we'd never met, a wealthy one

and so left without my sister

without you without her, me all by myself about to go mad i was

sick and tired of living a life

without tomris, iris, mesrop, efterpi, vangel, the farandole, i

easily fell for that handsome young man whose house was in a dead-end street over in our part of town

he was a musician who played a portable organ at local weddings

the organ had been passed down from his grandfather

his mother and father were the type of people who committed suicide together happily departing as one to the other side

leaving their son

with the organ and a roof over his head

my lover he lived in fener but in a neighborhood rather far from us

just you yourself and your motorcycle

“no need to think twice, he’s a catch, all alone like that, no relatives to burden you!” auntie meryem said.

uncle ferit had committed suicide in a strange way, according to the police at the station and to the papers too:

hanging himself by his belt from one of the springs of the mattress he slept on

and we were in mourning in those days

meryem and raggedy dwindling down to skin and bones

at our place day and night now

for a coffee a smoke fortune-telling

to warm themselves and fill their stomachs their heads hanging low

my mother, “well, seeing as you’re in love now ’bout time you flew off to build your own nest too; girls they want to know what it’s like having their own home!.. you’re smart! your life instincts are strong, your ego will protect you” she said hugging me and crying. but it was only herself she cried for anymore. uncle had been found dead in the street a few months earlier and mother was slowly fading away

you’ll stay here alone? i said... just look at how many we are here, she said, what do you mean alone!..

and then in what must have been an attempt to dispel the dismal-ish mood that had settled into the house upon my decision to leave she set up the gramophone and put on a record,,, she stood up, told me to join her,,, then, my head's spinning i can't,,, she sat down, her eyes closed.

"you can have baldy if you like, take him with you?" she said. and to that

"no way, it's just an apartment," i said, "it's no place for baldy!" and together we wept. that first marriage of mine would last a year. i'm going to write all about it in another book.

chapter two

so here you are,,, standing in the kitchen in front of the copper skillet,,, you've left those small sorrows behind. the death of your mother, your first husband the organ player, your career, your lovers,,, stalwart in your resolve you've made yourself forget all about those vehement times you dedicated to fixing society, the beatings you took,,, in each bout of loneliness you found him at your side,,, or he found you,,, zeyyat,,, you started out as someone who rebelled against the established order, and ended up defeating everything as part of that very same established order,,, but now they give you drugs that defeat your hatred,,, your self-loathing,,, "seroquel",,, "contramal," "ritalin," they're healing you,,, that's right, for years you grappled with the amorphous state of existence transformed into sociality,,, existence you said was revived within that magma,,, was it existence that came alive,,, what was it,,, that exists,,, did it come alive,,, the copper skillet,,, go take your pills,,, you usually chuck them into the trash when sabit isn't looking,,, why do you keep that man in your life,,, you see him as a kafkaesque character and take pleasure in his existence i suppose,,, there you go, still supposing,,, "know it" already,,, inside him lives a model of society that can never be changed,,, the model of society that you hate,,, that cannot be changed,,, sanctimonious,,, a model of society that certain people take pains to better by force though the society itself has no desire to change,,, a model of society for which wars are waged,,, lives surrendered,,, a rotten society which some strive heart and soul to change,,, that's gone to pot in the hands of its exploiters,,, sabit,,, could it be that you're the one exploiting him,,, could it be that you've projected your unsuccessful social struggle onto him,,, because you're old now, because you can no longer take to the streets, or join in the marches, you have taken that society into your home,,, you can't live without it,,, society stands before you right now,,, sabit,,, the enemy is inside your home,,, you are bound to one another by contract,,, you create one another,,, he sits with you, lies with you,,, eats,,, speaks,,, yet he gains nothing from you,,, he doesn't want to change,,, the other day he told you that he doesn't feel responsible for anything,,, responsibility,,, i don't buy into that philosophy,,, why should i be responsible for the lot of millions of ignoramuses,,, i'm the only person i'm concerned with,,, i take care to stand tall and not stoop to their level, he said,,, feeling responsibility for a people who have no desire to change is a ludicrous kind of dedication,,, it's not for me,,, he's content,,, he doesn't rebel,,, just wants to be left alone,,, he's never going to change,,, goddamn it you still pity this society you numbskull,,, you pity it,,, and sabit too,,, there's something they lack,,, you sense it,,, and they realize we have something they don't,,, that zeyyat and i have,,, what is it,,, the desire to seek the truth,,, or the desire to change oneself and others, maybe that's it,,, but now you're here,,, you're in the kitchen of an apartment,,, it's hot and you're sweating,,, you've dumped the semolina halva into the melted butter,,, you're stirring it,,, the kitchen door opens onto a small balcony where your husband sits on a thonet chair reading "le monde",,, he gets to read the papers before you do in the mornings, because you, as soon as you wash your face, you've got to throw on some clothes and make his breakfast,,, sabit,,, by the time he heads out onto the balcony, which he'll do shortly now, he expects his coffee to be ready,,, you never could understand why exactly,,, why hasn't it ever been you sitting over there and him over here,,, does he need you,,, is he ill,,, no no not at all,,, it's because he's ten years older than you,,, no no not at all,,, he's in better shape than you are,,, and he doesn't take any pills or anything,,, all day long he asks you whether you've taken your pills or not,,, plus he takes you to that dunce of a doctor, he's started graying around the temples,,, he's already lost the hair on his crown started balding looks less like a pop star now more like a gigolo who's been kicked to the curb,,, but he had those expensive new teeth made for himself, they're all the rage these days, and now his mouth won't close,,, pearly white asks:

"what are your hopes for the future?

do you feel guilty?

have you ever wanted to kill yourself?

do you often feel like crying?

do you hate yourself?

are you sick of everything?.."

yes, I am,,, i'm sick of everything and everyone including you you rat,,, SICK OF IT ALL,,, i love myself dearly,,,

i'm no crybaby,,, i can't tell you how many times i've wanted to kill myself,,, i've never felt guilty,,, as for the future, i'd like to see all the traitors croak before i die,,, so you're going to up the dosage for which one this time?

that's our life,,, that's how it is,,, he wakes up wanting his coffee,,, if you're late, it's now where's my coffee, is it too much to ask of you, for you to serve your darling husband a simple coffee,,, like he's the spoiled only child of the house,,, insists on playing the role of the beloved husband,,, constantly astounding you with his unwavering obstinacy,,, what do you mean astound the man drives you nuts,,, his morning coffee,,, lucky for you, you've no brain in that head of yours you say in a voice only you can hear,,, of course you don't want to hurt him,,, thinks you're nothing but a harmless madwoman, doesn't pay you any mind,,, oh but he does,,, he deems himself worthy of your mercy,,, sabit was always drawing birds as a child,,, perhaps that's why he ended up this way,,, that's what he said,,, come my son, she'd say to him, sit here and draw some nice pictures for mommy my love,,, first draw a bird and then color it in for me she'd say,,, for years he drew his mother flowers, birds, cats, streams, trees, all to prove his love for her,,, the poor thing,,, and his mother hung those clumsy drawings on the walls of their house,,, all the time he keeps saying, i loved tekir so much,,, and, i loved my mom so much,,, i was an obedient child,,, well, i obeyed my mother,,, i loved her most of all, more than my dad, more than anyone,,, that's the only secret he's ever shared with me,,, there's a huge portrait of his parents hanging in his study,,, his mother looks like a horrible woman,,, like a lion tamer,,, resembles uncle a bit too,,, she has a pretty face,,, looks a little like michèle morgan,,, her forehead's like a long, endless road,,, once sabit said he wished everyone loved him,,, i asked him why,,, because that's when i feel most at ease,,, his cat was a scratcher but really smart,,, like a person, he said,,, as soon as it sensed that sabit loved someone else it would immediately sink its claws into the object of his affections,,, i told him it was a good thing the cat was dead otherwise it would've been sinking its claws into me,,, and he replied, you seem awfully certain that you're loved, can you imagine,,, who would expect such a comeback from that dimwit,,, but zeyyat will be here in a little bit,,, i'll show you, i thought to myself...

how happy you were whenever your mother held you saying the pebble-birds pecked at my little girl's knees,,, the reason you'd make yourself slip on your way in from the garden and throw yourself down onto the pebble mosaics,,, uncle leaned down whispered in my ear, one day you're going to throw yourself out the window too,,, that devil of a man,,, could read my soul,,, long gone now thank goodness,,, they said the streets were covered in ice,,, he was on his way down standard-bearer street,,, saved me from becoming a murderer, the prick,,, but i'm not quite sure,,, sometimes i think i am a murderer,,, whenever abraham and isaac come to mind,,, so has murder entered thought or not,,, this sabit,,, he's never experienced real pain,,, real pain,,, i know it,,, and he's never had any problems either,,, you resent that too,,, it's as if he never even experienced the oedipus complex,,, he grew up without any fear of castration,,, he's unflappable and happy all the time,,, doggedly happy,,, and he's even happier when zeyyat's here,,, he trembles the moment he takes you in his arms,,, says, see, you're mine,,, a voice inside keeps telling me to leave him,,, make him miserable,,, this man who insists on being happy despite everything,,, what a disgusting thing, to be happy on this earth,,, it's as if he and his god are in an alliance of deception,,, take zeyyat and go,,, ditch him like a bad habit, leave him all alone in this house,,, take no pity on him,,, just get rid of him,,, he loves zeyyat too,,, and me as well,,, is that so,,, but you can't leave him,,, you aren't capable,,, he can't live without you, you know that,,, you're merciful,,, you're such a good person lahzen,,, as if,,, like they say,,, they put him in a coffin and sent him upstream alive and kicking,,, and the stream deposited him onto the shores of constantinople,, and from there someone who was the enemy of us both took him in and raised him, then entrusted him to you...

here's your nejcafé darling,,, you're using the letter j again have i upset you or something,,, of course not dear did i use a j,,, besides why should the letter j mean i'm angry,,, i didn't say angry i said upset,,, he's acting all spoiled and he knows it, how annoying,,, and you know that he knows it,,, if he knew what I was thinking,,, makes my cheeks flush, when he acts like this,,, here my love, drink your nescafé you say smiling,,, he smiles back,,, that j sound must come from the gendarmerie he says,,, the gendarmerie never did anything to me, i told you that,,, they kept me for questioning for a few hours then let me go,,, he thinks he's being clever, leading you into a dead end,,, you keep telling yourself to run off with zeyyat, that'll show him,,, it wasn't the gendarmerie that tried to fuck me it was this society you idiot...

or could it be that you're punishing yourself by not leaving this man,,, do *you get a taste of eternal torment from it,,, because of your crimes,,, which crimes though you're not really sure,,, how cruel you were to uncle,,, you didn't kill him but you might as well have,,, you constantly wished for him to die,,, if the prophet abraham is a killer well,,, then you,,, no no oh no don't get wrapped up in these anxieties,,, besides why should the prophet abraham be considered a murderer,,, wasn't it god who gave him the order: "*KILL*"? of course it's all because of those pills, they're to blame,,, it'd never occurred to me before,,, that* MURDEROUS GOD! GOD THE MURDERER! MURDEROUS GOD! *that's it!* MURDEROUS GOD! *zeyyaatt! if i were to tell sabit about this right now,,, he'd say don't be ridiculous, have you taken your pills,,, he's a sørenian too after all,,, the fact that god is a murderer doesn't negate the fact that abraham was isaac's murderer though,,, they're both executioners,,, forget about all that right now,,, just look at your husband, over there slurping his nej-café,,, your problems are the furthest thing from his mind,,, toss "the pill" in the trash while he isn't looking,,, zeyyat's going to be here soon,,, don't be trembling like a sparrow when he gets here,,, what's that sabit,,, i love you, that's what i meant to say,,, could it be that sabit's still in love with me,,, oh come on,,, the doctor must've told him to be nice to his wife, be understanding and all that jazz,,, okay but,,, you must remember that time he took a handful of pills and tried to commit suicide,,, that's right,,, of course,,, he knew he wouldn't die, that he'd be saved,,, he played that game too, trying to rope me into being his slave for the rest of his life,,, headed off my attempts,,, he's simply too cunning, you'll never beat him, you're well aware of that,,, he's been playing with you for years,,, you survive only by ignoring him,,, he knows it,,, there's something that he's clinging to,,, there is but it isn't you,,, you're not what he's clinging to,,, it's his own existence,,, his own existence,,, granted to him as an object,,, that's all he's interested in saving,,, you should up and leave one day,,, while he's asleep,,, you should do it,,, you shouldn't trick him,,, but he* *can't be tricked anyway,,, he's fine with it,,, i'm sure he knows everything already,,,*

– anything else you want, sabit?

– i want you! what are you doing?

– what am i doing,,, making semolina halva

– what do you mean, semolina! so it's the anniversary of şevket bey's death

– that's right, you know that?

– the tradition of dead generations descends upon the living in full force, isn't that so?

– what's that what did you say? i can't hear you from in here, raise your voice a little

– i said, the tradition of dead generations descends upon the living in full force

– i know you don't care for semolina halva but i've really no choice i'm sorry

– ...

– i think everyone likes semolina halva, including me, i wonder why you don't like it?

– i like the franciscans!

– good for you

– and our malamatis,,, you know running around with their cloaks and their canes,,,

– you mean to tell me there are still malamatis in this society? our muslims though, they sure have moved up in the world,,, cross the nouveau riche with ignorance and you get gluttony galore, that's what our muslims are like

– and thank goodness for that! we'd go hungry if the whole world were malamati,,, nothing would ever get produced!

– the ones these days don't produce anything either; i was referring to what remains of malamati belief in the existing system, not that i've given up on the concept of equality

– what does that have to do with anything?

– well this; here i am standing in the kitchen bored and exhausted cooking semolina halva for the sake of a tradition belonging to dead generations while you sit over there smoking your pipe and reading the newspaper!?

– oh come on!!! no one's asked you to make that halva!

– i know they haven't, but it also doesn't occur to you to lend your beloved wife a hand; i made up the beloved bit of course!

– how long's it been since şevket bey passed away?

– as long as i've been alive, i never saw his face

– did you get your ex to help you make halva too i wonder

– he was a madman you know that

– a nutcase, i thought you split up because he believed in god

– he was? pretty much the same thing when you think about it

– as long as you don't go leaving me because i don't believe in god!

– are you scared of something like that happening i do have to wonder

– well then keep wondering i'm not going to tell you

– that other one was a nutcase like søren! forget about him for now though, if you're harboring any regrets because of my past well once this halva is ready and i've had a rest then we can talk! but no, you keep me here stirring this halva nonstop my back aching while you lounge out on the balcony enjoying your pipe,,, i know you're saying all this not because you love me, not because you're jealous of my past, but because you're trying to put off coming over here and stirring this halva

– i'm not the one respecting tradition; should i have a guilty conscience because i'm enjoying my morning

– as if i believe in tradition

– that's what shocks me too; you don't believe yet you make halva for your father's soul?

– it's a whole different category, just drop it for now. are you coming or not?

– why should I?

– come and stir this so i can rest for a bit

– okay fine but there's one more thing i'm quite curious about

– all this talk just so you can put off coming over here but fine ask away

– so many revolutionaries have been killed yet not once have i seen you cook halva for their souls? there are thousands of them, sung and unsung

– i'm hardly in a state to go cooking semolina halva for all the revolutionaries of the world now am i!

– not all of them, the christians wouldn't want it anyway, their ashes would be writhing in pain! but what about the ones we knew?

– them? they didn't believe in stuff like this; they were activists; enough already are you coming or not? my arm's spent, my wrist hurts, i'm drenched in sweat, i need to change my clothes

– alright alright,,, i'm coming but this doesn't mean i'm making any concessions in terms of my thoughts, you can be sure of that

– if i only knew what thoughts you were referring to!

– have you forgotten, your existence is inherent to my own, and mine to yours!

> *hmph! look at that woman.*
> *it's like her father's spirit has risen from the grave and is watching to see if his daughter's going to hand out halva for him this year or not; pure insanity! more ridiculous than believing in god!*
> *she says she's going to change her clothes, she'll put on her red dress for sure, after all zeyyat's on his way isn't he!*

– don't go turning the heat up, you have to stir it patiently over a low flame, fifteen minutes more till it's done

– would you look at that! semolina halva, so demanding

– if you get impatient and turn the heat up thinking no one will be the wiser, you'll burn the nuts; we'll catch on to your trick, you can be sure of it!

– you don't trust me one bit; i told you i wouldn't turn it up and i won't, besides the gas is barely dribbling in these days; iran's about to cut it off altogether

– iran could open the valve all the way right about now, so you best keep a close watch on it

– you sound just like one of the ancient skeptics you know that right

– i don't know and i don't care. oh the good ol' days! nothing like grill charcoal now is there

– you mean wood charcoal

– there used to be a burst bag of charcoal leaning up against the plum tree in our yard,,, uncle used it to grill almost every day,,,

yirise se perimeno yirise

mikrula mu kopela

ela ela ela...

– that's all well and good but here you are about to honor the memory of uncle even, just because he knew how to light a grill, besides why haven't you ever danced the farandole for me

– at this age!

– true i'd forgotten you're a hag

– ...

– i'm sorry, alright but who in the world uses a charcoal grill anymore! you and your grilling,,, even greenpeace is losing the battle against technology that much is clear

– ...

– out there on their motorboats, releasing all that exhaust

– ...

– how beautiful you are my darling; that poppy color really suits you

– ...

– but i apologized, i was rude, forgive me. i know you're still young and captivating

– ...

– well suppose i am jealous!

– i'm absolutely shocked, shocked

– forgive me

– oh that mind of yours! you never did understand me

– i know; my mind, a bone-dry desert and all alone!

– with oases too that you've shut me out of!

– the doorbell

– i'll get it, you keep stirring

– i'll stir til zeyyat gets here, but then i'm done!

> *just look at that woman, what have i done to deserve this; i don't care for semolina halva, don't believe in traditions, never even met her father! she never met him herself...*
>
> *and look at how she runs at the mere mention of zeyyat's name!*

s– hello zeyyat glad you could make it

z– thanks sabit, have you seen the news? your people have banned entrance to taksim square on may 1st again

s– what makes them my people

z– just a turn of phrase dear,,, they say it'll provoke the public, and that the local shops will be vandalized!

s– as if everyone doesn't already know it's they themselves who're doing the provoking!

– ...

s– zeyyat come over here and stir this stuff

z– coming sabit, oh how wonderful it smells, is that halva, i love halva

s– today marks one hundred days since lahzen's father died!

l– don't get started again sabit,,, zeyyat stir it gently please, keep going till the pine nuts start to brown,

z– don't worry i've got it

l– zeyyat, you know that woman who works for us, zehra, the one who wears a headscarf when she's out in public but takes it off when she's in the house

z– ah yes that poor creature you mean? what's happened to her!

l– oh nothing,,, but the policemen from the security cabins at the hospital where her daughter vildan works have been following the girl home after work at night; their house isn't far from yours you know. vildan is scared to death, rushes home so fast she's out of breath by the time she gets there,,, her father waits for her at the end of the street every night,,, zehra's been asking me where she can lodge a complaint about the police, who she should tell,,, then she suggested, maybe you could tell zeyyat bey?

z– you want me to have a talk with them?

l– would be great if you could

s– aren't you guys a hoot, what on earth are you going to say to them zeyyat?

z– why do you say that sabit; i'll ask the chief there to do something about it

s– and how do you plan to introduce yourself? are you going to tell him that you're a friend of sabit bey's, that you're retired from the people's liberation party-front?

l– well in that case why don't you go and speak with him yourself sabit?

s– oh no, don't drag me into this lahzen; besides, what's the big deal, so the lads forget they're police when they see a pretty young woman, is that really something to get worked up about!..

l– not just yet!

s– tell zehra hanım to ask the hodja to do something, and to please not get us involved

l– what hodja?

s– which one do you think, whichever one she goes to

l– well isn't that just like you! always wriggling your way out of things

z– don't you two get started again please let's enjoy a nice sunday together

l– alright zeyyat darling, i apologize now just keep stirring and i'll heat up some milk,,, have you had your morning coffee yet?

z– i haven't but shouldn't you rest a bit first, you look tired

l– oh no i'm not tired at all

s– you're not tired huh!? then how come you were just chewing my head off a minute ago saying that you were!

l– i was talking about my wrists, and saying i was sweaty and bored

s– but one shouldn't be forced to do things they don't believe in now should they!

z– alright well i'm the one stirring now. stop arguing; so tell me, what's going to happen now that the provincial governor says he's not letting anyone onto the square on may 1st

s– who was it that said shorties are always tall on trouble

l– must've been someone tall like you who made that up sabit!

z– no no, i've heard it before too, such a saying does exist lahzen, well this sure is turning into a proper roux smells absolutely delicious! may it please your father, what a lovely tradition, you're going to pass it out to the needy too right!

s– but of course; for some reason his excellency couldn't manage to create a world without the needy! look here i for one am not budging, whoever wants to pass that stuff out can do it themselves; if that isn't the last straw!..

l– well that much is obvious dear, we only know two of our neighbors in the building anyway; zehra will pass it out tomorrow, and then i'll let her keep the rest

z– you mean there won't be any left for us? look here i plan to have a generous helping myself!

l– go ahead and eat as much as you want don't worry, there's plenty to go around; it's one of those bountiful dishes, you know, seems to multiply as you cook it, just look we have a giant cauldron full of it!

you'll have to wait a little while though let it really soak up the flavor then you and i can have some together

s– are we going to say a fatiha for your father's soul too huh lahzen

l– being a bit unpleasant now aren't you?!

s– marx sure knew what he was talking about, tradition truly has descended with all its might upon the shoulders and wrists of medieval turkey! i don't understand you lahzen! apori, apori! the great paradoxes of zeno,,, i'd prefer it if you believed in god; then i'd just say it's cause you've gotten old and been seized by the fear of death...

l– i must tell you sabit, i've had it up to here with this grand posturing of yours, there are emotions that your mind cannot not grasp,,, i've had enough; you don't allow for your own subjectivity, you go making fun of me to avoid revealing the real problem, the one that resides in you!..

> *just look at her, the old windbag,*
>
> *couldn't make anything of herself and so here i am stuck with her,,, no idea why i'm so devoted to her,,, she never could hold down a job either,,, took early retirement,,, but she sure knows how to lash out at me,,, can't say she's crazy but she's definitely missing a few marbles!..*

z– hold up! one minute lahzen, what on earth's going on, why are you getting so worked up darling, you two need to calm down; seems to me we're all forgetting where we came from; so we're trapped here in this country but let's not take our frustration out on each other,,, we'll have to suffer the consequences of being born here, just like everyone else. erase that awareness and next thing you know we're at each other's throats over some semolina halva,,, lahzen the milk's boiling over!

l– okay i turned it off. let me see, ooh! will you look at that! the pine nuts are beautiful, pink as can be! thank you for your help zeyyat, health to your hands. now i'll cover it and let it sit for a while... your coffee's ready shall we move to the living room?

s– well if you two will excuse me i'm going out for a little walk, hopefully by the time i'm back this place won't reek of semolina. i'll be back for lunch but i'm not having any halva... don't you forget to take your desipramine lahzen

l– don't worry i won't

so i'm thinking, how about i pack my bags and move into my aunt's house. it's empty and run-down,,, i could fix it up,,, put in pvc windows,,, laminate flooring,,, after aunt died they sent sultan to live with our bigbeargramps,,, they say the woman taking care of bigbeargramps sends sultan off to clean houses but keeps the money for herself,,, so how about i rescue sultan,,, have her move in, then she can take care of me,,, i could make myself comfortable on auntie's throne, the one in the room that overlooks the sea, and has a view of the palace's grand white landward entrance gate,,, how about i buy uncle hasan's buggy, hitch tralala up to it and drive it myself,,, uncle hasan's old now,,, how about i tell him all he has to do is take care of tralala, feed her, give her water, groom her,,, how about i put all my pills in a bag and toss them into the vortex of the whirlpool that's always there between küçüksu mansion and the pier,,, i'm not crazy or anything,,, how about i watch the whirlpool devour the pills,,, and i yell at the sea, saying you're not going to swallow me up anymore,,, and i return home,,, and sit in front of the window and get lost in continuous thought that nobody can interrupt,,, how about i start pondering again the substance of my truth,,, no i'm not going to think about my mother anymore,,, or my childhood,,, or my wacko lovers,,, not going to think about evil at all,,, i need to think about myself,,, i am whatever i am,,, how about i declare that this is me,,, and gradually reconstruct the meaning of existence within myself,,, how about i write a book about how no one in this world is able to be themselves,,, and i explain the reason for the lack of conscience in this country,,, how about i take only volumes of poetry with me, and it takes the rest of my life to read all of the poems of the world,,, how about i put sultan in the seat of the buggy, as the woman of the house,,, and i cover her legs with auntie's english plaid wool blanket,,, how about we go out to get fish from gani reis, over by the anadoluhisarı pier,,, and we grill out in the garden,,, swordfish, mackerel, turbot, bonito, anchovies,,, salad,,, how about we pick some eggplant from izzet's garden and smoke it on the coals,,, and i invite zeyyat over,,, and i tell him don't forget if i die before you do you're supposed to adorn my coffin with that purple kaftan,,, i want to live in this house with you,,, and i tell him sabit was toying with my very existence, that's why i left him,,, i'll pronounce it l'existence, that will really impress him i know it,,, the neighbors, my remaining relatives, they won't say anything,,, your voice, your sentences are tender, the red of poppies, humble, just like vangel's,,, how about i say, my love the lines of whose slender hands so resemble my own, i love you,,, i'm not going to read any more philosophy, i'm going to recreate the world from scratch all on my own,,, and i'm going to reconsider my take on søren,,, how about i say, i don't believe all that nonsense in the holy books either,,, especially not the ploys of positivist rational thought in the new testament, i never did fall for those,,, you know, the arguments between god and abraham,,, and all that stuff about abraham convincing god, definitely not buying it, how about i say that,,,

i'm not turning on the tv anymore either, not tuning into that man's no-god-but-me sermons,,, or his commands to worship him, to pray for his remembrance,,, how about i say let the idiots believe in that tongue of yours that's a rod then a snake like moses's staff,,, how about i confess that this society's primitiveness, its resistance to change has begun to spark joy within me,,, how about i say they'll understand only when they hit rock bottom,,, how about i say, zeyyat,,, why is it a salve to my wound that they remain unconscious of the fact that they're sick, maimed, evil,,, how about i say, am i an evil person too i wonder,,, and he and i ponder and debate this question endlessly,,, how about i afflict him with these thoughts he could never agree with,,,

how about i tell him to finally cast off compassion and feelings of kindness,,,

how about i tell him, actually, you're what's left of the me who failed to emerge from the past, from what was already given, but i still love you,,, and then later,,, how about i say that sabit can come visit us once a week,,, and one day there's a sudden knock at the door,,, and a fat blue-eyed wide-hipped woman walks in,,, and she says it's rosa lahzen don't you recognize me and she wraps me in her arms,,, and we weep together,,, how about she says that she's back for good,,, and we raise our glasses and laugh,,, how about zeyyat says to me, your laugh is so beautiful lahzen,,, and i say to rosa, come on let's teach zeyyat the farandole, you haven't forgotten have you,,, and she says, how could i ever forget,,, and the three of us wait like that together till the end for its arrival,,, and rosa asks whose arrival,,, and i say the revolution's,,, the revolution's!? she says, shocked,,, still, she asks,,, and i say yes, still,,, how about rosa says, in that case we better get to work,,, and i say okay, we will, won't we zeyyat,,, and he says of course we will, we're not dead yet are we...

List of Characters

abdullah çatlı

abraham: the convincer

abraham 1: isaac's murderer

abraham 2 : "what choice do i have at the command of my allah i'm about to give my child as a burnt offering to his path but isaac doesn't know what i'm about to do telling him would be tantamount to entrapping my allah, keep your voice down!"

adnan menderes

adorno

ahmet uzun

alaattin demirci

alis hanım: monsieur garbis's wife alis hanım went about dressed only in black, their house though was the color of indigo.

allah (jalla jalaluhu)

andon effendi: the only person our aunt laughed with

andrea doria

anthemios

antiochus: *long live* the infidel

antonioni

aphrodite

architect dimadis

aris usta: at number 11 in the mirrored arcade, but he never left.

aristotle

artemis

aunt: who lived in küçüksu / who said she loved me and my sister so much / who at every turn, scared us out of our wits,,, reminding us we were going to burn in hell / never once letting us forget about crime and punishment / or the afterlife!

aunt hafize: one of our aunt's neighbors in küçüksu

aunt lefkothea: my mother's dear friend, our "auntie roly-poly," efthim's mother

aunt meryem: raggedy mefkûre's mother

aunt saadet: can you spare a lemon,,,

aunt vara: sent us sweetbreads with vangel

auntie aliye: one of the women who rolled tobacco at the cibali factory

ava gardner

avram the tinsmith: one of our aunt's neighbors in küçüksu

aydın hatipoğlu: at the protest, beating the man who hit şükran in a flurry of mad punches

ayhan ışık

bakhtin

balyan effendi

barba-rossa

barber necati: one of our aunt's neighbors in küçüksu

bedros: at number 17 in the mirrored arcade, button-seller

belkıs abla: one of our aunt's neighbors in küçüksu

bekir: uncle's hunting buddy

bekir yıldız: coming to the protests by the star of his brow

bergman

bertolucci

bethuel: bethuel who had a todo bara gaze, rosa's daughter who died

bezirgân the banker: the noble, enlightened people of fener,,, they're all underground now

bigbeargramps: the one who never dies

blind şerif: a man they called the watchman of the mirrored arcade,,, who could perceive and see everything through sound

bogos: at number 18 in the mirrored arcade

buñuel

celâl bayar

charles boyer

charles vidor

circe

cobbler talip: in germany / lived and died a stranger to that country / a person without a past

comrade hrant

concord: oh how insatiable you are, wrapped in the arms of your first man, the future "strange man"

constantine

danielle darrieux

debussy

demeter

deniz gezmiş

dike

doğan öz

don quixote

edy: the park hotel pianist

efraim ezgin

efterpi: from our farandole troupe

efthim: my sister's first love

einstein

emine ocak

emine: one of the secret sect girls

empedocles

engels

enver pasha

erol taş

esau: hairy-handed, rosa's only surviving son

evliya çelebi

fahrünnisa: working for lüks nermin

faruk ersan

ferhat tepe

ferih egemen: our school took us to one of his plays "please take me along too / make me laugh till i cry / if i act out and upset you / you can beat me till i die..." / got pounded into our heads

ferit the coachman: pulls at the shrunken sleeves of his old jacket whenever he speaks,,, a wide-eyed oddball with a face covered in cracks like an aged oil painting,,, raggedy mefkûre's father

fikri sönmez

filly fatma: one of our aunt's neighbors in küçüksu. apparently only able to recognize each other from their shoes, they peered at one another's feet as they scooted from person to person falling into conversation all wearing old thick-soled shoes, it was they who were the first generation to suffer the full brunt of postwar life

fingerless hamdi

foucault

fransua: sarkis usta's son

freckled nahide: goddess of cuntery

freud

frisky: the horse aunt hitches to the buggy herself, the one leading us into infernal flames

garbis sarıcıyan: siranuş's father

gonca kuriş

grand sinan

greenaway

güngör dilmen: who writes about tourists eating brains at a live monkey restaurant

hadji murat: our three story timber house is the work of this greek craftsman. hadji murat, forced by religious persecution to travel to mecca from trabzon, and convert to islam, a master builder who engraved his name into stone, and carved the arches of domes, a christian in secret

hagar: ishmael's mother

haluk kırcı

hatice özen

hayrihünsa: one of the secret sect girls

hayriye: one of the secret sect girls

hazrat ali

herakleitos

hristo: the pleater, at number 16 in the mirrored arcade, brought the first pleating machine to turkey

hürcan gürses

hüseyin cahit yalçın

hüseyin inan

ibrahim çiftçi

ibrahim kaypakkaya

ilhan berk: it isn't until later in life that he sees istanbul for the first time; when he arrives here lahzen is in her twenties

irfan: who got rosa pregnant by holding hands when dancing the farandole

iris: together with whom we went looking for ego

isaac 1: new isaac, rosa's son who died

isaac 2: our rooster whom uncle murdered

isaac 3: born of sarah, to be sacrificed by abraham, who never questions but obeys, only senses, isaac is made of child-hues

isaac 4: we hunted it down instead of the boar, name's isaac! uncle said

isidore

ishmael 1: the rooster

ishmael 2: some say it was ishmael abraham was going to butcher

ivan the terrible

jacob: new jacob, rosa's son who died

j.-p. sartre

jesus

jirair: florist at number 20, in the mirrored arcade

john wayne

justinianos

kaidanovsky

kakoyannis

kemuel: new kemuel, rosa's son who died

kenan budak

kenan şengöz

khan bayezid the thunderbolt

kingfisher: who comes back with a massive sea bream

koço dimitri: at number 1, in the mirrored arcade

komet: now at number 10 in the mirrored arcade, a studio in the room between the goddess of bounty and the goddess of knowledge, komet who paints canvases with poetry and poetry with canvases

lahzen: who am i and what kind of person am i become / every day i ask myself where within my lived experience am i living / lahzen in which consciousness are you / from the clouds of which sky did you rain down / onto this wasteland tell me / seeing as the final consciousness shall be death / and the consciousness of consciousness at the moment of death cannot be written / at which junction of immaterial reality are you / i lahzen

lajos II

lars von trier

latif can

leucothea: hair drenching wet just emerged from the sea the girl from the marsh croft

liszt

lüks nermin: spinning the thread of life

lüks nermin: the madame of the famed bawdy house poverty girls would wind up in

madame hirsch: rosa's mother

maria palaiologina

marilyn monroe: this world of ours before whose mirrors / she floundered for years / until the kennedy brothers / destroyed / the visible part of her

marx

mayk: also a button-seller at number 19, in the mirrored arcade

mehmed the conqueror

mehmet sözer

melahat of çanakkale: goddess of mischief

mesrop: together with whom we went looking for ego

minotaur

mister achoo: our famous history teacher

moiz pizante: from whom mother bought a fez-colored robe de chambre for uncle, at number 13 in the mirrored arcade

monsieur garbis: a tailor for wealthy greek families

mother kıymet: one of our aunt's neighbors in küçüksu

mumcu

murat II

musa anter

mustafa kemal

münevver: the childhood love of the greek jeweler from istanbul

my mother (şehnaz): my mother's just a woman who loves the farandole,,, a self-contained being, more so than i am perhaps,,,

myrna loy

my sister (binnur): i don't have a father,,, he died just before i was born,,, i hug my sister every chance i get,,, it's okay, she says, don't worry, we've got our mother and our aunt too,,, and our great great-grandfather nobody can hurt us.

nâzım hikmet

necmettin büyükkaya

nevin şeref: musa's partner

nurettin: uncle's hunting buddy

oedipus

ohing

onat kutlar

orhan keskin

osman nuri uzunlar

our master the prophet (pbuh)

phanariotes: we're entranced by the starry language seeping through lives lived a-mingle

phony züleyha: goddess of the afterlife

pir sultan

plato

polanski

praefectus proclus

pulgher

rafael lami: at number 10 in the mirrored arcade

raggedy mefkûre: aunt lefkothea secretly took raggedy mefkûre there to cure her of idiocy

ramon novarro

rebecca: mute rebecca, rosa's daughter who died

reşit bey: and while we kids flirted with each other on his beach he, a tall fair-skinned communist youth, reşit bey of reşit bey beach, was rotting away in jail

rosa: whose face was vases of giggling freckles, my best friend

ruhi su

rupen usta: at number 15 in the

mirrored arcade

sabahattin: a satchel slung around his neck, trying to sell newspapers *sabah, akşam, tercüman*... aunt havva's son

sabit: my husband, whom i thought i was in love with,,, we'd kissed in the hippodrome,,, sabit's a good guy,,, never makes a fuss about my ex-lover,,,

sahure hanım: one of our aunt's neighbors in küçüksu

salih gevenci

sarah: isaac's mother

sarah: dark-browed and blue-eyed sarah, rosa's daughter who died

sarkis usta: at number 12 in the mirrored arcade

sefer yetzirah

selim the grim

semavi eyice

septimius severus

serdar alten

sevinç özgüner

shimmying banu of the tray: hugging sheaves of wheat

shirley temple

shrill ruhiye: goddess of the heavens

simento ruso: ended up moving to a building in the fish market together with rupen usta

sina kabaağaç

sinan suner

siranuş sarıcıyan: yarn seller in the mirrored arcade, with whom mother will have a chat,,, and in this way kind of teach us about our future lives.

socrates

søren kierkegaard: without casting off myth, religion, ideologies, matters of gender / the family / all the aggregates of social power / without being purified of the filth of these tsunamis / is it possible for a philosopher to arrive at a genuine theory? / at the truth of reality / the reality of truth / his essence and own substance / it is said that søren's real concern / was unseating hegel / please tell me dear readers / how does a thinker arrive at the crown gate of being a thinker / how does a thinker / arrive at wisdom / without first being purified / of feelings of animosity and envy

spencer tracy

st. augustine

st. george

sudsy mefkûre: goddess of love

suleiman the magnificent

sultan: an armenian girl living with our aunt who'd taken her in as a baby and raised her, she never knew she was armenian

sümeyha: one of the dark-skinned family girls devout and demure

suphiye: one of the secret sect girls

şahap bey: our turkish teacher

şükran kurdakul: who said, the meaning of life consists

of living for the sake of others unconditionally

tarkovsky

tayfun: from our farandole troupe

terfiye the shrew: goddess of music

the chechen miliski brothers: make fantasy bouquets and funeral wreaths for "the church of three altars," at number 21 in the mirrored arcade

the kantakouzenos: noble, enlightened people of fener,,, they're all underground now

the mavrocordatos: noble, enlightened people of fener,,, they're all underground now

the mavrogenis: noblemen, the enlightened people of fener,,, they're all underground now

the tekfur king

timur the lame

theodosios II

theseus

trickster zeus: witness to of the end of my first marriage

thutmose III

türkan şoray

uncle: being a man that no one knew my father was hiding in our house at one time, making mother forget about father,,, according to us, a strange man living in our house his face at times that of a workhorse at others a hyena and still at others angelic

a chimera of a hundred other beasts and men

uncle emrullah effendi: working for monsieur garbis as a baster

uncle haçik: beaten during the pogrom of september 6th and 7th left crippled then bedridden, father of mesrop

uncle hasan: there aren't any other drivers on this side of the bosphorus who have their own buggy and carriage. he's one of a kind our uncle hasan

uncle kosta: a karamanid turk, butcher, vangel's father

uncle petrus: the draper, efthim's father

uncle şakir the paralytic: he was paralyzed by a stroke yet recited the koran from where he lay, auntie aliye's husband

vâlâ nurettin

vangel: my boy lover / i'm still a child without you i haven't been able to grow up

vedat: taking rosa's hand making her feel as though she might faint, from the pleasure of it

vedat aydın

whip-wielding saliha: goddess of peace

wittgenstein

yahya kemal: sitting at the bar in park hotel, his huge ass spilling off the stool

yaşar gündoğdu

yaşar sucu

yervant: the piano tuner

yılmaz demir

yorgi: from our farandole troupe

yusuf aslan

yusuf the junkman: who'd willed that his bones be taken to israel when he died, rosa's father

zeyyat: my lover, the lines of his hands so like the lines of my own

Glossary

The aim of this glossary is to provide information about some of the references that are made in *What Remains* to particular people, places, myths, stories, and concepts that relate to the underlying themes of the book. Some of them may be familiar to readers, others may not. While far from being comprehensive, it may nonetheless serve as a rough guide through the rich social, cultural, personal, and historical topographies that Erbil weaves through the narrative. It was compiled entirely by the three translators and, since the original did not have a glossary, we can only hope that she would approve of its inclusion here.

"this book has never been submitted for any 'awards.'"
From 1968 onwards, Leylâ Erbil vowed to never submit any of her work to book awards or contests and included this statement at the beginning of all her published books.

"scurl up" (19)
A created word that attempts to echo the lexical playfulness of the Turkish. Erbil occasionally coined new words out of existing ones in *What Remains* (as she did in many of her other works).

tekel (19):
The Turkish tobacco, alcoholic beverages, and salt company, nationalized in 1925 from the Ottoman parastatal company the Régie. TEKEL was the sole manufacturer and distributor of all alcohol and tobacco products in Turkey until being sold to the British American Tobacco company in 2008, following privatization. In 2009 the factories were shut down resulting in one of the most widespread general workers' strikes in Turkey.

"*yirise se perimeno yirise*
mikrula mu kopela
ela ela ela..." (19):
The chorus lines from a Greek tango titled *Yirise, Se Perimeno Yirise* from 1947, by lyricist Nikos Fatseas and composer Giannis Vellas. In the song a young man pines for a long lost lover, asking her to return. Erbil uses these chorus lines: "Come back, I am waiting for you, come back" (Γύρισε σε περιμένω γύρισε), "my little girl" (Μίκρουλα μου κοπέλα), and "come on" (έλα έλα έλα) as a refrain that repeats throughout the Proem section in *What Remains*.

"*eho mono pono*
yirise..." (20):
"All I have left is grief / come back," (έχω μόνο πόνο / Γύρισε), lyrics from the song "Yirise."

çelebi (30):
An Ottoman-Turkish honorific corresponding to master or gentleman, used for educated and learned people.

balyan effendi (31):
Could be referring to any one of the many members of the Balyans, an Armenian family with many revered architects behind numerous prominent buildings and structures of nineteenth-century Istanbul.

hafize / hafiza (33):
A female name from the Arabic root "h-f-z" meaning "to protect" or "to conserve." In this context, it refers more specifically to people who have memorized the Koran, called "hafız" (for men) and "hafize" (for women) in Turkish.

"eyes full of rage
like silvana mangano's in *rome, open city*" (36–37):
In his blog post titled "zeyl," meaning addendum or supplement in Ottoman-Turkish, dedicated to clarifying in part certain idiosyncrasies and in part musical and film references Erbil makes in *What Remains,* writer Caner Fidaner explains this particular reference to the actress and the film as an accident of memory. That, in fact, it is not Silvana Mangano who plays the leading role in the film, but Anna Magnani. And that it is Magnani's eyes that are "full of rage" when she sees her fiánce captured by the Gestapo in a famous scene from the film.

madame "lüks nermin" (40):
Nickname of famed brothel owner Şaziye Zeren Topçu, who ran brothels in Istanbul starting in the 1940s and continuing until her retirement in the 1980s, reaching the height of her fame in the 1950s. She was known as "luxury Nermin" thanks to her reputation for welcoming customers by offering the most luxurious of items, as well as providing high-ranking sex workers to extremely high profile customers, especially government workers and diplomats. She reached the pinnacle of

her fame amidst scandal, when the president of Indonesia at the time learned he had syphilis after engaging the services of one of the sex workers employed by Lüks Nermin, which lead to a diplomatic crisis between the two countries, and to Nermin's falling out of favor with, and into the crosshairs of, the government that had protected her so diligently up until that time.

semavi eyice (47):
(1922–2018) Renowned historian, especially noted for his knowledge of Istanbul.

andrea doria (48):
(1466–1560) Genoese statesman and one of the leading naval commanders of his time, he played a key role in the Republic of Genoa, to which the medieval citadel of Galata belonged between 1273 and 1453. He hailed from a famous, influential Genoese family, whose connection to Galata predated the foundation of the republic, as the city-state of Genova too had strong ties to the city even before the Ottomans took it. The coat of arms referenced here is actually three coats of arms side by side: the coat of arms of the Republic of Genoa, featuring the cross of the republic's patron saint, St. George, flanked by the coat of arms of the Doria family on the left, and the De Merude on the right. Although this is the most famous Andrea Doria, previous family members also bore this name, so the coat of arms belongs to the ancestors of the Andrea Doria that Erbil references in subsequent lines.

burnt gate (45):
Said to be a gate opened in the city walls of Constantinople in 1335 in order to contain a fire, though it is also said that there was already a gate in the same place predating the Galata Tower (507–508 AD). No remains survive of this gate though the name Burnt Gate is frequently used in place of another gate mistakenly, Harup Gate (also Harip Gate), which still stands on Burnt Gate Street and which bears the three coats of arms mentioned in the entry above.

todo bara (52):
A reference to silent movie actress Theda Bara (1885–1955), commonly referred to as Hollywood's first femme fatale.

"followers of nur" (58):
The Nurcu (in Turkish) movement, also known as Followers of Nursi, is an Islamic community movement founded in the early twentieth century in Turkey, based on the writings of the Kurdish Islamic scholar Said Nursi (1876–1960). The movement divided into several fractions following Nursi's death. The most influential faction was the "neo-Nurcu" movement of Fethullah Gülen (1941–2024), which became organized and institutionalized in Turkey (and internationally) by establishing educational institutions and gaining a powerful presence in media networks and civil society organizations. Gülen and his supporters had close ties with the AKP (Justice and Development Party) and Recep Tayyip Erdoğan, aiding the AKP's rise to power. Though the movement thrived during the time AKP was in power, a rift between the two became apparent following corruption investigations led by a Gülenist judiciary in 2013 of high-ranking AKP politicians. The conflict seemed to have reached its peak when the AKP linked the coup attempt in 2016 to the Gülen movement, and officially named it (abbreviated "FETÖ" in Turkish) a terrorist organization.

raised pavement street (65):
A street in Istanbul starting from Galata and ending in Karaköy, once famed for its brothels. Until the 1950s the street bore the typical Genoese characteristics of steep stairways found in the neighborhood.

"stones of iniquity" (48):
Stones feature prominently in *What Remains*. The author, the narrator and the protagonist are (we are told) in search of the truth that is hidden from view amidst the ruins and debris of catastrophe that is the history of "civilizations," the human greed for absolute power to rule and the unsteady nature of personal memory, specifically one that

has experienced trauma. Stones seem to be witness to and material of this zeal for power and the cycle of destruction and reconstruction it generates and everyone and everything it touches. It has been argued that stones are at the heart of the traumatic poetics in *What Remains* as well as other works by Erbil. At times, the narrator's death drive seems to be transformed into an urge to be one with the stones in an attempt to return to a past that has been traumatically cut off.

remzi (65):
Turkish publishing company founded in Istanbul in 1927 by Remzi Bengi.

"half a pencil is worth forty years of friendship" (66):
Erbil here makes an allusion to a well-known Turkish idiom about friendship that more or less means no matter how small an act of kindness might be, companionship is enduring: "Bir fincan kahvenin kırk yıllık hatrı var." This literally means a single cup of coffee is worth forty years of friendship.

ruhi su (66):
(1912–1985) Armenian-Turkish opera singer, folk musician and saz player. Su travelled extensively in Anatolia compiling folk songs and was active in the Turkish Communist Party. He was arrested in 1952 and imprisoned for five years.

yahya kemal (70):
(1884–1958) Turkish poet, author, politician, and diplomat born as Ahmet Âgâh and known by the pen name Yahya Kemal Beyatlı. During the reign of Abdulhamit II he became active in anti-regime movements and after fleeing to Paris to avoid arrest in 1903, he returned in 1912.

sina kabaağaç (73):
(1924–1997) Professor of philology and classics, son of the renowned Cretan-Turkish author Cevat Şakir Kabaağaçlı, known by the pen name "the Fisherman of Halicarnassus."

"live monkey restaurant" (74):
The title of a satire written by Turkish playwright Güngör Dilmen (1930–2012). The play takes its name from a restaurant the protagonists visit in Hong Kong in order to sample a revered delicacy: fresh brains of living monkeys.

"ena boukali mastika" (75):
Greek for "a bottle of mastiha," a sweet, mastic liqueur.

time-keeper street (75):
"Time keeper street," in reference to a room inside a mosque used by the timekeeper, the clock room, where a visible clock was placed for people (on the outside) to observe the time through the windows of the room.

farandole (52):
An ancient folk dance from Provence and Catalonia said to be related either to the medieval carole or to be of Greek origin with a link to the "cranes' dance" attributed to the myth of Theseus and Ariadne: "On his voyage from Crete, Theseus put in at Delos, and having sacrificed to the god and dedicated in his temple the image of Aphrodite which he had received from Ariadne he danced with his youths a dance which they say is still performed by the Delians, being an imitation of the circling passages in the Labyrinth, and consisting of certain rhythmic involutions and evolutions." The dancers link hands on both sides, form chains, and follow the steps of the leader through a serpentine course. The dance is accompanied by pipe and tabor players.

september 6th and 7th (76):
The Istanbul pogrom (also known as Septemvriana) that took place on September 6 and 7, 1955, was a series of state-instigated mob attacks against the Greek community in Istanbul in which the Armenian and Jewish communities were also attacked. The Turkish press, in the lead up to the centrally organized riot, had been stirring up extreme

nationalistic, xenophobic sentiments and on September 6 the publication of a fake news story in the paper *İstanbul Ekspres* contending that the Turkish Consulate in Thessaloniki was bombed by Greeks was followed by organized crowds gathering in districts around Beyoğlu the same day. By the afternoon and continuing into the next day, the mob started destroying non-Muslim owned shops and attacking houses, churches, schools, and cemeteries in districts with Greek, Armenian, and Jewish populations. The riots were later revealed to have been orchestrated by members of the Democrat Party (whose founder Adnan Menderes was the prime minister at the time), the government (the president at the time was Celal Bayar), the Turkish military, and the police in coordination with the "Cyprus is Turkish" Association (KTC). The pogrom has never been officially denounced nor have there been any compensatory legal damages awarded for the losses suffered by the various individuals and communities.

yeşilçam (78):
This is the name of a street in the district of Beyoğlu in Istanbul where the offices of most film companies were located prior to the 1980s. Now it is a metonym for the Turkish film industry as well as a particular era in Turkish cinema, which had its heyday between the 1950s and 1970s.

ayhan ışık (78):
(1929–1979) Born Ayhan Işıyan, known in the press as the Crownless King, an actor and producer and one of the most popular leading men in Turkish cinema.

türkan şoray (78):
(1945–) Actress, writer, and film director, known as the "Sultan of Turkish cinema."

erol taş (78):
(1928–1998) Famous supporting actor, usually cast as a villain in Turkish cinema.

"their turbans
kavuks
sarıks
üsküfs
upon its artüres" (95):
Carved stone embellishments placed on the top of tombstones in Ottoman cemeteries. They are particular to Ottoman culture in the Muslim world, taking the shape of various kinds of men's headdresses designating either the social or official rank of the deceased. The last on the list, "artüre," is a reference to the artist Yüksel Arslan (1933–2017). Born in the district of Eyüp in Istanbul, Yüksel Arslan's oeuvre is deeply connected to literature and writing. Artüre-Arture is a self-coined term with the addition of the French suffix "-ure" to the word "art," which the artist began to use to refer to his artworks following his move to Paris.

"yallah, yallah yallah min ruh, to havariyyun, to havariyyun!.." (100):
"Onwards, onwards, onwards, believers, to Havariyyun," which was the site of the Church of the Holy Apostles, a Byzantine Orthodox church in Constantinople. The initial building was constructed in the fourth century and future emperors added to it. The church was second in size only to Hagia Sophia. When the city was taken by the Ottomans in 1453, the Church of the Holy Apostles housed the Ecumenical Patriarchate of the Eastern Orthodox Church for a short time but then it was allegedly abandoned. In 1461, the remains of the Church of the Holy Apostles were torn down by the Ottomans to make room for the construction of Fatih Mosque.

"(the kingfisher we mention being none other than horoz
captain of büyükada
remembered always
together with sina and selah)" (109):
Berç Yetvart Akdeniz, known by the nickname Horoz Reis or "Captain Rooster," (1926–1978) was a well-known fisherman from Büyükada, one of the Prince's Islands. He was famous for his kindness and

dedication to helping the locals of the island. Even in the roughest weather, he would sail people who were ill to the hospital and help find fishermen who were lost at sea. See also the entry for Sina Kabaağaç.

küçükçekmece lake (115):
A lagoon located on the European side of Istanbul.

phanariotes (115):
The Phanariotes were members of one of the leading Greek families of Phanar (Fener), a Greek quarter of Constantinople, who served as administrators in the civil governing class and held a great deal of power in the Ottoman state in the eighteenth century. Some of them had become quite wealthy in the sixteenth and seventeenth centuries and used that influence to bolster their positions in the government.

evliya çelebi (123):
(1611–1682) Evliya Çelebi, whose true name was Dervish Mehmed Zilli, was an Ottoman explorer. For forty years he travelled extensively around Ottoman territories and outlying areas, writing down his impressions and observations, which would be published in a book called the *Seyahatname*, or *Book of Travels*. His travels took place at a time when the Ottoman Empire was at the peak of its power and expansion.

karamanid turks (124):
The Karamanid Turks were part of the Salur tribe of Oghuz Turks who started migrating westward from around the area of modern-day Azerbaijan due to conflicts. By the fourteenth century they had established a powerful dynasty in central Anatolia.

"ayrılık belki ölümden beter..." (125):
Literally "Separation Is Perhaps Worse than Death," this was the title of a song by a well-known Turkish singer named Şecaattin Tanyerli (1921–1994), whose compositions were often inspired by tango music.

"picnic grounds in dört kardeşler" (132):
Dört Kardeşler, or "the Four Siblings," was a meadow near the shores of Göksu Creek, which flows into the Bosphorus near the district of Beykoz on the Anatolian side of the city. As a picnicking area, it was popular because of its proximity to fresh water springs, which were used to make lemon-flavored soda and other beverages. The area was named after a large plane tree growing there that had four large trunks.

"don't make me come after you with my slipper!" (139):
In reference to a tradition that is common across the region, threatening to throw or actually throwing one's slipper at someone is seen as a means of berating or punishing them.

potur pants (144):
Baggy trousers that are cinched in at the waist and taper down around the ankles. Often seen as being a traditional, conservative form of attire.

şükran kurdakul (145):
(1927–2004) Born in Istanbul, Şükran Kurdakul was a Turkish writer, poet, and researcher. When he was in high school, he was arrested for carrying out communist propaganda and imprisoned for four and a half months, for which he was expelled from school. While he was working as a teller at a bank in 1953 he was arrested again for engaging in communist propaganda.

aydın hatipoğlu (145):
(1940–2010) An author, playwright, and poet, Aydın Hatipoğlu published his first poems in 1958 in a magazine run by Şükran Kurdakul. In 1971, one of the publications he was running was shut down under martial law.

bekir yıldız (145):
(1933–1998) A prolific author, Bekir Yıldız grew up in various places around southeastern Turkey, where his father worked as a police

officer. In 1966, he published his first novel and proceeded to publish a large number of short stories, which have since won awards in Turkey. His works tend to focus on the lives of people living in the southeast of Turkey.

"*ayda to moro mu*
hayda to yavri mu
den ta tu to foreso ali mia" (151):
"Come on, my love
Come, my sweet.
O, I'm lost and forlorn without my lover."
Song in a dialect that is a blend of Turkish and Greek, of unknown date and origin.

maksim nightclub (151):
The Maksim Nightclub, located near Taksim, was open from 1921 to 1927 and then again from 1961 to 2005. The building, which was constructed in 1914, was designed by Giulio Mongeri, an Italian architect. In 1921, a foreigner by the name of Frederick Bruce Thomas rented the large lower hall of the Cinemajik Theater and transformed the space into Maksim Nightclub. The nightclub, which featured the first performances of jazz musicians in Turkey, quickly grew in fame and became a popular place for dances such as the foxtrot and the charleston.

ragıp pasha mansion (151):
Built in 1906 for Ragıp Pasha, an influential merchant who held various positions in the Ottoman government, the mansion is located in the district of Kadıköy on the Anatolian side of Istanbul. The architect was August Carl Friedrich Jasmund, who also designed the Sirkeci Railway Station. The mansion, which has three main buildings, has changed hands numerous times since the death of the pasha in 1920. It was used for a while by the Istanbul Sailing Club and for a period of time it served as a military jailhouse.

sanasaryan han (154):
Constructed in 1895 and named after Mıgırdiç Sanasaryan, a wealthy Armenian merchant, the notorious Sanasaryan Han was initially used as a means of generating income for Sanasaryan College in Erzurum. The five-story building is located in the district of Sirkeci in Istanbul. The han was confiscated and repurposed following the Armenian Genocide, and during the occupation of Istanbul during the Armistice period of World War I, it was used as the headquarters of the British, who transformed the basement into prison cells. In 1937, the building was transformed into the headquarters of the Istanbul Police Department. It was during this time that Sanasaryan Han began to acquire its reputation as a brutal center of torture, as political prisoners were held there during the state's crackdown on communist activities. Sometimes prisoners were held there for weeks and months on end in what came to be known as "the torture chambers," which were cells that were so small that prisoners could not even sit down. Writers, artists, and poets who had ties to communist groups were held there, including such figures as Nâzım Hikmet. In 1945 it was alleged that one political prisoner had died as a result of the torture to which he was subjected but the police claimed that he had leapt to his death from the top of the building.

iş bank coin bank in taksim (162):
A large clock in the shape of a coin bank that was located in Taksim Square.

fahrettin kerim (163):
Fahrettin Kerim Gökay was a mayor of Istanbul in the 1950s known for his intolerance of alcohol consumption. Locals started ironically referring to small bottles of rakı as "Fahrettin Kerim" as a dig at him.

emil galip (163):
(1922–1993) Emil Galip Sandalcı was a journalist and writer. At one point he was arrested and jailed following the military memorandum

of 1971, during which time he was tortured. Galip launched a signature campaign to prevent the execution of Deniz Gezmiş and his associates. He was later imprisoned again by the state following the military coup of 1980.

"... like all loves will this too come to an end, i wonder..."
"*... her aşk gibi bunun da bilmem gelmez mi*
Sonu..." (168):
Lyrics from the song "Mehtaplı Bir Gece" ("A Moonlit Night") by Seyyan Hanım (1913–1989).

"you fled like a seagull longing for distant coasts
far from the shores of my heart, from the horizon of my eyes..."
"*uzakları* özleyen *bir martı gibi kaçtın*
gönlümün sahilinden gözlerimin ufkundan..." (168):
Lyrics from the song "Bir Martı Gibi" ("Like a Seagull"), also by Seyyan Hanım.

vâlâ nurettin (169):
(1901–1967) Also known by his pen name, Vâ-Nû, Vâlâ Nurettin was a journalist, translator, and writer. He penned some of the first detective novels in Turkey. He was close friends with Nâzım Hikmet and after travelling from Istanbul to Anaolia to support the Turkish War of Independence, the two of them went to Moscow together to study. Upon returning to Turkey, he worked for a number of different newspapers.

letters from my windmill (169):
A collection of short stories by the French writer Alphonse Daudet that was first published in 1869.

"the rowboat rises / the rowboat falls" (169):
Lines from a popular poem titled "The Caspian Sea" by Nâzım Hikmet (1902–1963).

ferhat tepe (172):
(1974–1993) Ferhat Tepe, who was a Kurdish journalist and correspondent for the Bitlis office of *Özgür Gündem*, was disappeared in July 1993. Tepe's tortured body was found thirteen days after his abduction in the vicinity of Lake Hazar near Elazığ.

musa anter (172):
(1920–1992) Also known as "Apê Musa," Musa Anter was a Kurdish writer, journalist and intellectual. He was assassinated by JİTEM (the Turkish Gendarmerie Intelligence and Counter-Terrorism organization responsible for extrajudicial killings, torture, and forced disappearances in the 1990s) in Diyarbakır.

vedat aydın (172):
(1953–1991) Kurdish politician and human rights defender. He was abducted from his home, tortured, and disappeared. His body was found under a bridge in the district of Maden in Elazığ province.

yılmaz demir (172):
(?–1984) Kurdish revolutionary who hanged himself in a final act of resistance to stop the torture being carried out at Diyarbakır Prison. He left a message explaining his act: "I am sacrificing myself so that torture will cease at jails and so humane conditions of incarceration will be implemented."

fikri sönmez (172):
(1938–1985) Fikri Sönmez was a Turkish communist politician who served as a mayor in the district of Fatsa in Ordu province. He was targeted by Prime Minister Süleyman Demirel during the Çorum Massacres. He was later arrested and imprisoned at the Amasya Penitentiary and died following a heart attack.

sinan suner (172):
(?–1980) Sinan Suner was a student at ODTÜ University in Ankara

when he was shot during an event in which activists were putting up posters supporting the revolutionary cause. The shooter was Süleyman Ezendemirby, who worked as a security guard for Cengiz Gökçek, a MHP minister. He was then abducted, tortured, and left for dead at the entrance of a hospital.

ahmet uzun (172):
(1957–1981) Ahmet Uzun was one of the first volunteers involved with the Revolutionary Path movement in Rize, where he was born. While the Revolutionary Path movement was based on Marxist-Leninist tenets, it rejected the Soviet political model, opting to support a more Turkish-based approach. All the same, as a communist group, it was violently suppressed by the government. After the military coup of 1980, Uzun was captured by government forces following a series of clashes in Rize and imprisoned. He died as a result of the torture to which he was subjected during his imprisonment.

alaattin demirci (172):
(1957–1981) Born in the Black Sea Region of Turkey, Alaattin Demirci became actively involved in the Revolutionary Path movement in the town of Rize, where he attended high school. While he was engaged in militant activities near the town of Artvin, he was killed by government forces.

kenan şengöz (172):
(1955–1981) While Kenan Şengöz was born in Bitlis, he ended up working as a finance clerk in the Black Sea town of Rize, where he was involved with the Revolutionary Path movement and took part in anti-fascist activities. Following the military coup of 1980, he played an active role in events geared towards opposing the junta, first within the town of Rize and then in its outlying areas. Cornered by state forces, Şengöz and his companions fled into the mountains, where they were involved in clashes with the gendarmerie. Due to the snowy conditions at the time, they froze to death in the higher reaches of the mountain range.

hatice özen (172):
(1957–1978) While she was a student at Istanbul University, Hatice Özen, who was involved with the revolutionary anti-fascist movement, was one of the thousands of people who lost their lives during the course of clashes that were taking place in Turkey between leftist and far-right groups in the 1970s. As the decade wore on, the conflict became increasingly violent. On March 16, 1978, as Özen and a group of her friends were leaving a building at Istanbul University, they were ambushed by members of a far-right group, who attacked them with gunfire and a hand grenade. It has been alleged that the police had been tipped off about the attack but waited for it to take place before showing up at the scene. Özen, who was a third-year student at the time, died in the attack along with six of her classmates.

palilalia (174):
Palilalia is a rare speech condition that involves the involuntary repetition of words, phrases, or sentences, often becoming faster and quieter with each iteration.

kallikantzaros (175):
In Southeast European and Anatolian folklore, the kallikantzaros is a malevolent creature that is generally nocturnal. It is believed to live underground but comes up to the surface for a fortnight starting on the winter solstice. For the most part, they are imagined as being small, dark-colored humanoids with animal-like characteristics. Often they are imagined as being blind. In some places, they are thought to have a foul odor and be fond of eating small creatures such as worms and frogs.

"kamer çehre peri-ru / tende canım
nigarım, dilberim, ruh-i revanım
enisim, sim-berim yar-i vefadarım..." (175):
"Face comely as the moon, visage of a fairy, my darling in the flesh
My beloved, pretty as a picture, mate of my soul

My companion, silver-breasted, my dearest, always true..."
Song originally composed by Hacı Arif Bey (1831–1885).

alaturka (175):
Music (or other cultural expression) in a traditional Turkish style, as opposed to Western style (or "alafranga").

abdullah çatlı (176):
Hitman for the Turkish intelligence service, MİT. Aligned with the far-right Nationalist Movement Party (MHP), he orchestrated many political assassinations, especially against members of Kurdish and Armenian movements, both within Turkey and abroad. He died in the Turkish town of Susurluk in a car crash alongside several prominent political figures in what became known as the "Susurluk scandal," which blatantly revealed the connections between elected and appointed officials and members of the "deep state" such as Çatlı.

mhp (176):
The MHP, or Nationalist Movement Party, is an ultranationalist political party. Established in 1969, the party is alleged to have connections to organized criminal organizations and paramilitary groups. The party's youth wing played a major role in the political violence that caused large-scale social upheaval in Turkey in the 1970s.

ibrahim çiftçi (176):
Far-right nationalist hitman for the Turkish government. He was tried for murder four times and acquitted each time at highly publicized trials.

haluk kırcı (176):
Far-right nationalist hitman for the Turkish government. He was arrested and imprisoned several times but was always released, despite having been convicted of multiple murders.

hasan ocak (180):
A teacher who also ran a tea house in Gazi, an Istanbul neighborhood largely populated by Alevis, a minority in Turkey. Thirty years old at the time, Ocak was disappeared in the aftermath of what would become known as the "Gazi Neighborhood Massacre," which took place on March 12, 1995, when fire was opened on three cafes and a patisserie from a passing car. When people took to the streets to protest, a total of twenty-two people were killed and some three hundred injured. The perpetrators who were identified got off with minimal if any sentences. Ocak's relatives searched for him for fifty-five days before finally finding his remains, which had been buried in a forest in another part of the city. He had been tortured to death. After Hasan Ocak's body was found, a group composed of people searching for family members who had been disappeared and who wished to call the government to account decided that they would sit silently, holding photos of their disappeared loved ones, in front of Galatasaray High School, a famous school on Istanbul's most prominent pedestrian road, Independence Street. They would become known as "the Saturday Mothers" and their silent protests would continue for decades despite attempts by the police to disperse them.

emine ocak (180):
Hasan Ocak's mother, whose tireless efforts led to the discovery of her son's remains and who helped establish "the Saturday Mothers."

yajuj majuj (182):
Arabic for Gog and Magog, which is Hebrew.

hınkır mınkır (182):
A supernatural evil creature from Anatolian folklore and Turkish mythology which is said to strangle people to death and then eat them.

tekfur palace (184):
Late thirteenth-century Byzantine palace originally known as Palace

of the Porphyrogenitus, commonly referred to by its Turkish name, Tekfur.

cobbler talip (31):
(1901–1983) Ahmed Talip lost his mother at the age of three and was orphaned when his father died in the War of Gallipoli in 1915. While at an orphanage that also acted as a vocational school, he was part of an agreement struck by the Ottoman Empire's Enver Pasha, whereby Enver Pasha asked to send between five and ten thousand male orphans aged twelve to eighteen, whom the Ottoman Empire claimed they did not have the resources to take care of, to Germany, which agreed to take around seven hundred children. Some, such as Ahmed Talip, were among the first to be sent, and they went on to work as apprentices. Records show that as many as forty percent of the children soon ran away due to poor working conditions, as many were made to work grueling hours for food and board alone. Ahmed Talip would end up becoming "heimatlos," or without a homeland, when the Ottoman Empire collapsed and the Turkish Republic was established, for he was still a foreigner in Germany, but Turkey did not claim him either.

comrade dink (184):
Reference to Hrant Dink (1954–2007), also known simply as "Hrant," a prominent Turkish-Armenian journalist and outspoken human rights activist. He was assassinated just outside the headquarters of *Agos*, a newspaper established in 1996 that was published in both Turkish and Armenian, of which he was editor-in-chief until his death in 2007. At the time, he was being prosecuted under Law 301 for "insulting Turkishness" due to a comment he had made about the Armenian Genocide, claiming that the outcome of historical events clearly revealed them to be nothing less than genocide, a claim that is illegal to make in Turkey. Right-wing, nationalist propaganda made Dink a target, while the state neglected to provide for his safety despite the numerous death threats he received, culminating in his assassination. Photos of his body on the sidewalk, covered by newspapers, only the

worn soles of his shoes visible, would imprint themselves on the memory of the nation. In 2010, the European Court of Human Rights found that Turkish authorities had violated Dink's right to life by not acting to prevent the murder and by not punishing the police for inaction.

yaşar gündoğdu (185):
(1956–1980) Kurdish leftist who was tortured to death.

sevinç özgüner (185):
(1928–1980) Leftist activist who was shot to death, along with her husband, at their home. Their murderers were never found.

onat kutlar (185):
(1936–1995) Turkish writer and poet. Died of wounds incurred in a bomb attack at the Marmara Hotel's cafeteria. The attack was later found to have been carried out by the Kurdish Workers Party (PKK).

mumcu (185):
Refers to Uğur Mumcu (1942–1993), a Turkish investigative journalist killed by a bomb placed in his car outside his home. He was investigating the PKK's ties with the Turkish National Intelligence organization (MİT) at the time of his assassination. There are countless hypotheses and conspiracy theories about who was actually behind his murder.

doğan öz (185):
(1934–1978) Turkish jurist who was serving as the assistant public prosecutor of Ankara and investigating the ties between the counter guerilla movement and the deep state when he was assassinated one morning on his way to work. The shooter was İbrahim Çiftçi, a member of the right-wing nationalist Grey Wolves. Though he was tried and sentenced to death, the verdict was overturned and he was acquitted, a decision which even Çiftçi refused to accept, saying he would not walk and they should kill him.

orhan keskin (185):
(1956–1984) Kurdish leftist revolutionary captured by police in an armed clash in 1980. He was sent to Diyarbakir Prison, which was infamous for torturing inmates. Keskin joined the resistance within the prison to stop the torture, including participating in an indefinite hunger strike in 1983. When promises made to end that hunger strike were not kept, another hunger strike began in 1984, just days before Keskin was to be released. Keskin died on the fiftieth day of this hunger strike.

necmettin büyükkaya (185):
(1943–1984) Kurdish leftist revolutionary tortured to death during the Diyarbakır Prison Hunger Strikes (see entry for Orhan Keskin).

ibrahim kaypakkaya (185):
(1949–1973) Turkish Alevi leftist who founded the Turkish Communist Party/Marxist-Leninist. Following the military memorandum of 1971, which led to a crackdown on the communist movement in Turkey, Kaypakkaya and his comrades were attacked by Turkish military forces in the eastern province of Tunceli (Dersim). Kaypakkaya was left for dead but he actually survived, and eventually took refuge in a nearby village, where a schoolteacher initially took him in but then turned him over to the military. He was arrested and taken to Diyarbakir Prison, where he was questioned and tortured for four months before being shot and killed by military forces. His death, however, was officially ruled a suicide.

puro soap (187):
Turkey's first domestic, industrially produced toilet soap. Production began in 1952, and the soap remained on shelves into the 1980s. The soap also features in popular historical memory for an advertising campaign whereby tiny wrapped bars of the soap were dropped from airplanes.

yavedut sultan (189):
"Ya vedud" is one of the ninety-nine names for Allah. It literally means "beloved" or "most worthy of love" and "he who loves his creatures." There are many legends surrounding the sultan who came to be known by the name Yavedut Sultan and its connection with the sweating column. It is said that the sound of someone calling out "Yâ Vedûd" could be heard coming from the column, even when it was still a church. The source of this voice was said to be that of a dervish named Şeyh Maksud who disappeared inside the column during a visit while accompanying an officer who, with permission from the Byzantines, had come to the city to bury the Muslims who had died during the latest siege. When the ultimate siege fails to result in the Byzantines' defeat as quickly as Mehmet the Conqueror assumed it would, he is told that his victory cannot be sealed so long as Yâ Vedûd remains alive, but he is praying inside the column for Islam to conquer the city in fifty days. Mehmet conquers Constantinople on the fiftieth day, and upon entering Hagia Sophia, he and his entourage find a body facing Mecca and emanating light, with the name "Yâ Vedûd" written in red across it.

Other legends offer explanations for the column's healing powers. One claims that the column is from the home of Mary, Mother of Jesus. When she heard about Jesus being caught and tortured, she began to weep, and a teardrop fell onto the column she was leaning on, boring a hole into it that exists to this day (and is supposed to make wishes come true when you stick your thumb in it and turn it clockwise). Another variation on this legend is that during one of his frequent visits to the church during its construction, the emperor Justinian got a headache and leaned against the column, and his headache soon disappeared. Upon inspection he saw that there was a hole in the column, and a tear coming out of the hole. He thought this was the tear of Mary, Mother of Jesus, that had been sent by God to heal him. The people heard about this miracle and from then on considered the column sacred.

nikos gounaris (189):
Greek singer of popular music who was widely popular in the 1950s.

sofia vembo (189):
Greek singer and actress (born in Gallipoli) who rose to particular fame around the time of World War II.

maria vincent (189):
French actress and singer who sang on stages in Turkey frequently in the 1950s and the early 1960s.

ilhan berk (49):
(1918–2008) Turkish modernist poet associated with what is called the "İkinci Yeni" ("Second New") poetry movement.

aznavur arcade (193):
Built in 1894, this well-known arcade located in the Beyoğlu district of Istanbul takes its name from the Ottoman Armenian architect who designed it, Hosvep Aznavur. Aznavur was born in London but immigrated to Istanbul with his family as a child. He studied in Rome before coming back to Istanbul where he built several of the city's best-known structures. He died in Cairo, to which he fled following the Armenian genocide.

"... the european arcade, which an armenian named ohing had the italian architect pulgher design in pera in 1874, is in the neo-renaissance style..." (107):
The European Arcade, which is located in the district of Beyoğlu close to Galatasaray High School and the Beyoğlu Fish Market, stands at a place that once was home to the luxurious Naum Theater and the Jardin des Fleurs Hotel, both of which burned down in the Great Beyoğlu Fire on June 5, 1870. The architect who designed the arcade, Domnico Pulgher, who is known as an Italian architect but was actually born in what is today Austria, lived for years in Istanbul, where he designed and built numerous well-known structures, including the building that now houses the Consulate General of Sweden. The European Arcade, the roof of which is partially covered in glass for the

sake of illumination, also came to be known as the Arcade of Mirrors (Aynalı Pasaj) because at night gas lamps were placed in front of the famous mirrors that hang on its walls.

hazzopulo arcade (200):
Located on Independence Street in the Beyoğlu district of Istanbul and opened in 1871, this arcade was named after the Greek merchant or banker (sources are conflicted over this) who commissioned it. It is located just a couple hundred meters from the European or Mirrored Arcade.

öküzbaş laundry blue (200):
By the 1930s, the brand Öküzbaş had become one of the most popular bluing agents in Turkey. Originally made by a British company, eventually it started to be produced in Istanbul, which prompted the producer to claim that it was a "national brand."

melahat of çanakkale (202):
Name of a brothel owner in modernist poet Ece Ayhan's eponymous poem "Çanakkaleli Melahat'e İki El Mektup ya da Özel Bir Fuhuş Tarihi." It is uncertain whether she actually existed or not, but she is depicted as a tough woman who, though disenfranchised, refuses to bow down to social pressures and political forces.

"the girl from the marsh croft" (203):
The Girl from the Marsh Croft is a book by Swedish author Selma Lagerlöf, published in 1908 and adapted to film several times.

"the church of three altars" (212):
An Armenian church built in 1810 and located inside the fish market in the Beyoğlu neighborhood of Istanbul.

"kopsi kefali" (212):
Greek, meaning "off with the head."

tan (213):
Left-leaning Turkish newspaper published from 1935 to 1945. Anti-fascist and pro-Soviet, the paper called for greater democratization of Turkey, which included demanding an end to single-party rule as the People's Republican Party (CHP) remained the sole party in Turkey at the time. Most media outlets were openly pro-CHP and also propagated its policies, which included increasing alignment with pro-U.S. policies. When government-aligned newspapers targeted *Tan,* claiming they were trying to undermine the government and spread communist propaganda, a group of right-wing Islamist students marched to the newspaper's offices and raided and destroyed them. *Tan,* along with several other publishing houses and newspapers, therefore was forced to cease operations. One prominent journalist who targeted *Tan* was Hüseyin Cahit Yalçın.

hüseyin cahit yalçın (213):
Journalist, writer, politician (1875–1957). In 1908, he, along with two others, founded the newspaper *Tanin,* which espoused the views of the Committee for Union and Progress (CUP). During what would become known as the Uprising of March 31 of 1909, the offices of *Tanin* were raided and destroyed, and an attempt was made on Yalçın's life.

şan cinema (213):
Built in 1953, this beloved institution of Istanbul was damaged beyond repair when it caught fire in 1987. Although officially attributed to a problem with electrical wiring, many believe the fire was an act of arson carried out by right-wing conservatives in response to the play *Muzır Müzikal* ("*The Obscene Musical*"), which was critical of the conservative obscenity laws of the time.

atatürk cultural center (213):
Located in Taksim Square in Istanbul, the center was originally known as the Istanbul Palace of Culture, and opened its doors in 1969. It

was heavily damaged by a fire that broke out during a performance of Arthur Miller's *The Crucible* in 1970. Several leftists were eventually accused of starting the fire, though later tried and acquitted. It was later revealed that the Artists' Union had petitioned the public prosecutor's office, saying that two days before the fire, a group was handing out fliers signed by the Theater Censorship Committee, which demanded that plays which were not pious or nationalist be removed from the stage. The Union published a statement in response to this flyer, and asked the prosecutor's office to provide their members with protection.

madımak hotel (213):
A hotel located in the province of Sivas in central eastern Turkey. Musicians and other artists and intellectuals, mostly belonging to the Alevi minority, who were in Sivas to attend the Pir Sultan Abdal Festival, were staying at the hotel when a right-wing mob attacked it and set it on fire on July 2, 1993, resulting in the deaths of thirty-seven people inside. This would become known as the Sivas Massacre or the Madımak Massacre.

pir sultan (213):
Pir Sultan (Abdal) is an important religious figure in Alevism, believed to have been born in Sivas and to have lived in the fifteenth and sixteenth centuries.

ferih egemen (214):
(1916–1978) A Turkish actor, director, and author, he was best known for writing, directing, and acting in children's plays.

gospodars (217):
From "gospodar," a word of Slavic origin meaning "master."

emek cinema (218):
Cinema located in the Beyoğlu neighborhood of Istanbul, a local favorite and known for its baroque architecture. Emek showed films from

1924 until 2013, when it was torn down to make room for a new shopping mall, despite popular protests.

aşkale labor camp (219):
A labor camp in Aşkale, which is in the province of Erzurum in northeastern Turkey, where taxpayers unable to pay a wealth tax ("Varlık Vergisi") implemented in 1942 were made to perform hard labor on behalf of the state. The tax targeted non-Muslims in particular.

apurum (226):
Word used by the Göktürks to refer to the Eastern Roman Empire, or Byzantium.

puriam (226):
"Pure" in Latin

"porom" (226):
Possibly a reference to the song "El Porompompero," a Spanish song which became very popular in Turkey too in the 1960s. It comes up here presumably as a tool of alliteration.

"the junta of march 12th" (234):
The junta of March 12 is also referred to as the "coup by memorandum." The second military intervention to take place, it occurred in 1971, just eleven years after its predecessor in 1960. In the memorandum, the military delivered several ultimata to the government, which it saw as acting incompetently in suppressing a rising wave of socialist organizing at the time. As a result, the government cracked down on left-wing militants and activists in particular.

deniz gezmiş (234):
(1947–1972) Turkish Marxist-Leninist revolutionary, student leader, and political activist. He and two other members of the People's Liberation Army of Turkey (THKO), Hüseyin İnan and Yusuf Aslan,

were arrested on March 4, 1971, and charged with kidnapping four U.S. army privates for ransom as well as robbing a bank. On October 9, they were sentenced to death for trying to overthrow the constitutional order and executed by hanging on March 30, 1972.

hüseyin inan (234):
(1948–1972) See entry on Deniz Gezmiş.

yusuf aslan (234):
(1947–1972) See entry on Deniz Gezmiş above.

hızırilyas, or hidrellez (234):
Hidrellez is the name of a holiday celebrated in Turkey to mark the arrival of spring. It also honors a folk hero called Hızır. It is also said to mark the day when Hızır and another folk hero, İlyas, meet each year. Some therefore believe the name of the holiday comes from a combination of these two names, "Hızır" and "İlyas." Beliefs surrounding this holiday are manifold, with roots extending into Anatolian folklore as well as Islam and Christianity.

"wonders of creation" (234):
Kitāb 'Ajā'ib al-makhlūqāt wa-gharā'ib al-mawjūdāt (*The Wonders of Creation*, or, literally, *The Marvels of Things Created and Miraculous Aspects of Things Existing*) by Zakarīyā Ibn Muḥammad al-Qazwīnī (1203–83). The work is considered to be the most famous Islamic cosmography.

akdamar church (234):
Armenian church built between 915 and 921. It is located on an island in Lake Van in eastern Turkey.

danishmendid (234):
Turkoman dynasty that ruled over much of what is now central northeastern Turkey from 1071 until 1178.

"eûzü bi'kelimâtillahittammâti..." "min şerri mâ haleka..." "ve zerae" "ve berae ve min şerri..." (235):
Arabic prayer declaring that one takes refuge in Allah for protection from the devil and evil.

menderes (76):
Adnan Menderes (1899–1961) was prime minister of Turkey between 1950 and 1960. He was tried and hanged under the military junta after the 1960 coup d'état. His government was accused of being behind the pogrom against the Greek ethnic minority in Istanbul in 1955, in which thousands took to the streets to raid and destroy Greek homes, businesses, and churches in retaliation for a bomb that had supposedly been planted at Atatürk's home in Thessaloniki.

celal bayar (76):
(1883–1986) Prime minister of Turkey from 1937 to 1939 and president from 1950 until 1960.

painter komet (237):
(1941–2022) Turkish artist and poet whose real name was Gürkan Coşkun. He later assumed the name "Komet," meaning "Comet." One of the most important artists of his time, he was known for his fantastical allegorical scenes.

"lebon's cakes" (237):
A reference to the famous Lebon Pastanesi, a cafe and pastry shop on Independence Street in Beyoğlu, Istanbul. It was opened in 1886 by the Frenchman Edouard Lebon, a chef working at the French Embassy in Istanbul (then Constantinople). It changed location and ownership (and was closed and reopened) several times over the years before finally closing down completely in 2022.

"evliya çelebi travelogue" (237):
(1611–1684) Ottoman explorer who recorded forty years of travel

through Europe, the Middle East, and North Africa in what remains one of the longest, most detailed works of travel writing in any language.

çiğli (242):
A district of İzmir, a major city on the Aegean coast of Turkey, and home to Çiğli Air Base, a military base used by U.S. troops between 1959 and 1970.

"christos anesti" (245):
A traditional Greek Paschal greeting in Eastern Orthodox Christianity meaning "Christ is risen."

"alithos anesti" (245):
Response to "Christ is risen," meaning "Truly he is risen."

psito (245):
Traditional Greek dish, particularly in Thessaloniki, consisting of baked or grilled lamb or beef served with herbs and spices.

yavrimou (245):
A word meaning "my dear" or "my darling." It is a combination of Turkish and Greek. It melds together the Turkish word for "dear," "yavru," and the Greek for "my," "mou."

gonca kuriş (248):
(1961–1999) [Alternative spelling: Konca Kuriş] Turkish Islamic feminist who was openly critical of misogynistic, patriarchal interpretations of the Koran. She was disappeared in July of 1998. Her body was discovered 555 days later in January of 2000. She had been abducted, tortured, and killed by Turkish Hezbollah.

meyhane (163):
Traditional Turkish restaurant, much like a taverna, where alcohol,

generally the anise-based liquor rakı, is served along with various mezzes and seafood dishes.

asmalımescit (250):
A part of the neighborhood of Beyoğlu in Istanbul.

burnt castle (251):
Literal translation of the Turkish name for the city of Győr in northwest Hungary. During the Ottoman occupation of present-day central and eastern Turkey (1541 to the late seventeenth century), Győr's commander thought it would be futile to try to defend the town from the Ottoman army, so he burned it to the ground. The Ottoman forces arrived to find the city burnt to ruins, and therefore named it "the Burnt Castle."

malamatis (263):
A Sufi, or Muslim mystic, group that flourished during the eighth century. Their doctrines were based on a reproach of the carnal self and self-blame was a central tenant of their beliefs. They strove to be virtuous yet conceal their virtue from others.

One of the most influential Turkish writers of the 20th century, **Leylâ Erbil** was an innovative literary stylist who tackled issues at the heart of what it means to be human, in mind and body. Erbil ventured where few writers dared to tread, turning her lens to the tides of social norms and the shaping of identities, focusing intently on emotional conflict, and plumbing the depths of history and psyche. In 2002 and 2004 Erbil was nominated as a candidate for the Nobel Prize in Literature by PEN Turkey. She died in Istanbul in 2013.

Alev Ersan is an artist, writer, and translator based in Istanbul and Paris. Recent solo and collaborative work and publications include *Still in My Quotidian*, De Appel, Amsterdam (2024), *this contamination, and this crossroads, this accident here*, DEPO, Istanbul (2023), and *Radiant Absence*, Monograph for Füsun Onur, Istanbul/Milano (2022).

Amy Marie Spangler hails from southern Ohio but has lived in Istanbul, Turkey, for over 25 years. Co-founder and director of AnatoliaLit Agency, she also translates, mostly from Turkish into English.

Mark David Wyers completed his BA in literature and his MA in Turkish Studies. The author of a historical study about the interconnected issues of sex work, urbanism, and nationalism in Istanbul in the early years of the Republic of Turkey (from around 1923 to 1935), he has translated a number of short stories and novels from Turkish into English.

www.ingramcontent.com/pod-product-compliance
Lightning Source LLC
Jackson TN
JSHW021709100925
90242JS00002B/2

* 9 7 8 1 6 4 6 0 5 4 0 1 5 *